Kai Hayes is an amazin
ter life; one with promise, ...p. ....
not contain her: she is ever growing, ever becoming better. Catch the "winds from her sails" and let her lift you to greater understanding as to how you can change your life. I met Kai though our mutual dedication to a cause we both embrace: changing health and changing lives. She was a speaker for one of our events. As I watched and listened, I knew this was no ordinary woman. As we got to know each other better, we became friends. The richness of our friendship and common goals in helping people achieve better lives have been so rewarding. She is just beginning to climb towards her destiny - as great as the achievements of the past, I expect to see even greater achievements as she is determined to bring as many people as possible along with her. She cares about them and she loves her wonderful husband and son with a fierceness and dedication rarely seen in our present time.

Jacquelyn Sheppard
Author, Researcher, Educator, Counselor

I have had the distinct honor and pleasure of knowing my dear friend, Kai Hayes and her husband Greg, for almost a decade now. Their mutual love, admiration and support of each other, is beautiful to observe, and sets a benchmark for other couples.

Kai and I share the common passions of challenging ourselves to be better every day, while obeying God's calling on our life, and to significantly blessing others, daily. This brought us to the same international organization, which we proudly serve in a leadership and mentorship capacity. Kai has an absolute love of LIFE, as divulged by her infectious smile. It blesses me greatly to tell you about my dear friend, Kai!

To know Kai is to know pure human potential! She has worked tirelessly and sacrificially for every single accomplishment, break and blessings in her life. Kai knows adversity, but not how to quit. When she pursues (hunts) something she values, she doesn't let up until it has been tracked, bagged and tagged. Kai knows struggle, but not how to settle. She aims high and hits the mark. Kai knows failure and defeat probabilities, yet she just doesn't care. She makes obstacles, her workout routine. This book is the up-close and personal journey of her life, in all its terror and triumph. This is her story of faith, trust and VICTORY. This book is her gift to the world and your roadmap. Buckle up and enjoy the ride, because GPS won't help you. Help yourself and read on!

Dr. Dondee Nettles, DC
Entrepreneur, Podcaster, Wellness Advocate, Director of Wonderful

When I first met Kai Hayes, it was from a distance of about 30 feet. I was teaching a seminar on creating time and financial freedom in Austin, Texas, and Kai was dead center in about the tenth row and all I could really see was her bright eyes and beaming smile. When the class reached the Q&A portion at the end, she peppered me with insightful questions and great posture. She was a dynamo in the making for sure! Once the seminar ended, a select group was invited to join us for dinner and Kai came along. She sat directly across the table from me and that is where I started to learn just how much energy, passion and commitment this woman was pouring into her life and the lives of those around her.

Over the next 9 years our paths crossed many times as we became great friends and business partners. I learned of her difficult upbringing in the Philippines and how she conquered all the obstacles in her path leading her to Austin, Texas. I have been honored to be mentoring her from a distance as she continued to pour her passion and soul into her charity work, her marriage to Greg and the lives of those who grabbed onto her coat tails and said "I want what she's going after."

Her story in *Lion at Heart* will bring you to tears and elevate your soul all at the same time. Having said that, she's nowhere close to being finished. The journey she's on will continue to benefit her and the lives of those around her as she shares and cares for them all. I am blessed to call her my friend.

Greg Dieker
Entrepreneur & Leadership Freak

Lion at Heart tells a story of a true hero and her journey to overcome obstacles in life. Kai Hayes is a role model who will inspire you to push through the hurdles that prevent us from growing and becoming truly remarkable human beings.

Kai has taught me and thousands of people around the globe how to rise above our current situations, identify the mindset of a winner and "do" the activities that bring us growth and financial success.

Kai has become a very close friend over the years. I believe while she has already overcome so many obstacles and become an inspirational leader; she is only beginning to make her impact on the world. Kai's story, "Lion At Heart" will start a new revolution to empower people all over the globe to breakthrough their own barriers and create a life of their dreams.

Marc Shinsato
Global Business Entrepreneur

LION
at
HEART

Discovering Courage and Greatness Within

KAI HAYES

LION at HEART
Discovering Courage and Greatness Within

Copyright © 2020 KAI HAYES

Published by: Kai Hayes Lifestyle LLC

ISBN: 978-0578-6823-4-1

Dedication

To Jesus, my father, my son and my husband

In the vastness of the hardships and struggles along my life's remarkable journey, it is of utmost joy and bliss to honor and dedicate my book to the four men in my life: **My God and my Savior Jesus, my father Cristino "Nino," my son Nico "Isko" and my husband Greg.** *I wrote this book for all of you who have given me true strength and courage to walk through darkness and find greatness within. In you, Jesus, I became an expert in prayer during times of calm as much as I became an expert in times of crisis. For I discovered that the God I meet in good times is the same God who meets me in the hard times. Cristino, for your unconditional love, guidance and protection. For teaching me to discover courage and greatness within. For being there to face my perils with vigor. Nico, for fulfilling my utmost desire to become a mother. For being the biggest inspiration in my life, finding meaning in my existence, and face agonies in life with courage. And Greg, for allowing me to love again, to discover a new meaning in life, for supporting me along with all my endeavors to no end, for lifting me up when my heart is distraught, for being my strong pillar to lean on.* **My LOVE for you all will live forever.**

Table of Contents

Foreword

As I look back on my heroes – those individuals who have had a profound effect on who I am today, who have given me wisdom and guidance that has been invaluable to my success – they all have one thing in common: they saw extreme difficulties and challenges as a doorway to something great.

Kai Hayes is just such a person.

She has experienced profound difficulties and, instead of giving into them or simply ignoring them, Kai has used them to fuel her success. Because of that, what you hold in your hands is more than a book. It is a guide on how to see hardship as an opportunity and discover that you are … a "Lion at Heart."

As CEO of a $250 million publicly-traded company, nearly every day I see examples of people letting the difficulties of life stunt their growth. They shut down, shut off, and give in to the deadly victim mentality. In today's world this is more prevalent than ever. Kai's message could not be more timely.

In her signature heartfelt and vulnerable way, Kai has woven together personal stories, lessons and reflections to help you turn life's break**downs** into powerful break**throughs**. The key is to recognize things for what they truly are, transform the way you see the world, and discover that you have always been a "Lion at Heart."

Darren Jensen,
President and Chief Executive Officer
LifeVantage

Acknowledgements

I acknowledge all these men and women who have been a great part of my life journey – individuals who acknowledge that the world can become a better place. Believing that when we educate people and help them reach success, we achieve the best of humanity. I thank you all for leading and developing others, for inspiring and providing me the foundation to lead others and for everyone who strives to grow and aspire to become a better version of themselves. Without the experiences and support I had with all of you, I would not be where I am today.

I am extremely grateful to Darren Jensen for writing his profound and meaningful foreword. Thank you for the trust and endorsement. Jackie Sheppard, for your amazing mentorship, for being my adviser as I wrote this book, and for staying late nights with me for the final editing of my manuscript. Dondee and Marci Nettles, for helping me to be who I am today. For your continued support and inspiration. Greg Dieker, for always being there when I need your guidance and wisdom. Marc Shinsato, for your support and mentorship. You all have become dear friends and special part of my life. I am eternally grateful to all of you.

A very special thanks to my family & friends who are dear and special to me:

Agnes Dacono, Amy Holmwood, Anthony Krashowetz, Daniel Moellering, Antonio Quintos, Arlene Dockery, Becky Buhler, Bert Debroisse, Buddy Gomez, Cathy Anderson, Dr.Chad Luxemburg, Cioney Franke, Sr. Cynthia Camuta, Debbie Kral, Dr.Deborah Viglione, Dinah Rasdas, Eddie and Irene Lee, Edgar Avelino, Elsa Villagomeza and Gilbey Amaguin, Emman Avelino Fr. Edward Koharchik, Dr.Gene De Lucia, Grant Hayes, Jason Verdera, Kerry Florie, Kim Koebensky, Lourdes Lee, Marcia Livingston, Sr. Mary Ann Mc Fadden, Michelle Burmeister, Dr. Nancy Brian, Olive Carlos, Precioso Perlas, Precy Mercx, Roberto and Leah Gonzales, Rosa Avelino, Ryan Torkelson, Sam and Vandee Flake, Susan Go, Susie Caraway, Zach Padgett.

To all individuals I have had the opportunity to lead, or be led by, thank you for being my inspirations:

Andres Mandujano, Angela Bates, Ann Cubarrubia, Anna and Eduardo Larrazabal, Barbara Buchle, Beth Busa, Betty Pickard, Beverly Hills, Brandon Williams, Cheryl Cook, Christianne DeMoro, Emmie Cadavez, Evelyn Aquino, Gary Knight, Gigi Donohoe, Ivy Howard, Jackie Britt Kilby, Jacy Angelle, Jan Villanueva, Jane Anderson, Joe Fagan, Kara Petron, Kay Lenhoff Castro, Lily Cortez, Lourdes Bradford, Mamta Ganesan, Marjorie Ham, Martina Gamez, Mary Coop, Melissa Stockman, Millette Perez Jane Anderson, Natalie Stone, Paulette Schnipke, Rhona Talusan, Richard and Vickie Perales, Robert Duran, Rob Kabeiseman, Rosa Rivas, Sherry and Bob McDonald, Sylvia Morales, Tim Wait.

Lastly, extending my gratitude to my book coach, Alicia Dunams, my ghost writer Maggie Mills and my publishing manager Toccara Ross along with the whole publishing team.

I want to thank EVERY ONE of you who ever believed and trusted in me and said anything positive to me or taught me new things. I heard it all and I am grateful.

I want to thank GOD most of all, because without GOD I wouldn't be able to do any of this.

It was a true honor and privilege to work with all of you. This journey of writing my book, *Lion at Heart*, has given me the opportunity to know myself in a much deeper and meaningful way. It urged me to ask the Lord to grant me a Holy heart that is not concerned with the thing I call "myself," but instead to give me a sense of humor and find happiness in life by serving others.

Lion at Heart
Discovering Courage and
Greatness Within

Be Moved. Be Found. Be Changed.

Introduction

What is Life? How do you define *your* life? Is there something missing in your life? Do you like where you are? Do you like *who* you are? What is your purpose? What makes you happy?

Most of us ask these questions of ourselves at some point, but do we ever find the answers? More importantly, do we find the answers that make us excited to get up in the morning?

I've been asking myself these types of questions since I was a very young child. Now, I want to help you do the same soul searching, by sharing my story.

I wrote this book to help you and the people I love and care about. This book is also to honor the most important woman who ever lived on earth – Mother Mary. She is also the most overlooked amongst women. When we celebrate Mother's Day, there is very little to no mention of Mother Mary. So, I make a special point to mention her, for Mother Mary is by far the perfect example of a **"Lion at Heart."**

Mother Mary exhibited the greatest courage a human could ever have – the courage to take a challenging journey of the most excruciating pain any human being can possibly endure. She had a lifetime of struggles, humiliation and poverty. Yet, her faith and belief gave her the extraordinary power to endure, to face, to lead, to change the world. Mother Mary was a young woman who showed complete obedience to God and set aside her own desires for the sake of our Savior Jesus Christ. She is the epitome of a courageous leader who every woman must follow, for in her beats the heart of a lion, a true warrior.

At a very young age of 25, I began my difficult and challenging life journey. However, I believed that life is meant to be lived. My resiliency allowed me to make it this far. My real-life experiences led me to brave the unknown. Adversities visited me in winter, spring, summer and fall, yet I chose to discover courage and greatness within.

One of the most devastating experiences I had in life was in year 2014, when affliction visited my family. It came like a thief in the night. My husband, Greg, was diagnosed with grade 3 brain cancer. I needed every ounce of strength, every bit of determination I had, to guide our family during these challenging times. It was then that I discovered that despite being five feet tall, I had a lion inside me. A lion resided in my heart. A lion burst forth and roared with pain, and fear, and hurt, but mostly determination. I looked to the life of Mother Mary and drew from her example of compassionate strength and surrender.

The image of the lion dates back more than 30,000 years. The male lion, with his large mane, is a symbol of strength. The lioness combines her strength with a fierce maternal love. While the male lion protects the pride, the lioness hunts to feed the pride. The lion will leave the pride after two or three years, and the lioness remains with the pride throughout her lifetime. The symbol of the lion is embraced by all cultures as one of strength.

In the C.S. Lewis classic, *The Lion, the Witch, and the Wardrobe*, Aslan, the lion, represents the death and resurrection of Christ. The lion is the Christ consciousness within all of us. When my husband became sick, I realized that the lion had always been within me, and it was time to willfully release that power.

In this book you shall learn how to look into your heart. If you do, you will certainly discover passions and drives in your life that you wish to live for. You have the capacity to hate or love, to give or possess, to build or destroy, to forgive or avenge. But when you choose what is positive and shun what is negative you will naturally discover what model to embrace. And only then, you will discover the meaning of life.

My story from poverty to financial freedom is not mine alone. I did not work hard and endure hardships to keep my story a secret, for my story can help others, like you. My story may help you answer the questions: What type of life do I want? Who do I want to be? Who am I fighting for?

This book is for you – for those of you with wounded hearts, who are searching for answers to your prayers, hoping to improve your life. For those of you who want to improve your life. This is a journey to discovering your greatness and finding the courage to thrive.

As you read these pages, you will discover your own strength. You will discover the only person who can change your life is the person you are looking at in the mirror each day. You will discover your own worth, your own value on this earth.

You will eliminate the things that are insignificant in your life and begin to focus on what will help you achieve success. For what we focus on is what we get. The world needs your voice. You need to be felt, to be seen. Decide to be visible. Tell yourself you are invisible no more!

You will discover that we are all called to do great things, yet in order to do so we need to find a way to help others, for helping others leads to greatness!

You will learn:

- The way to map the road to your personal success.
- Inner strength is found during struggle.
- There is joy behind pain.
- How to unleash your greatest potential.
- The tools and resources for empowerment.
- How to achieve and create the lifestyle you've dreamed of.
- Ways to develop the proper mindset to break through barriers.
- Who you really are!
- What you are capable of achieving!
- The most important things on earth are people.
- There is a lion within your own heart.

I am very thankful for my past experiences, for they have shaped me well. So, I say to you, never disregard your hardships. They will give you strength and compassion for others.

I lived this story. It's real. It's a real journey to success. I didn't steal this story from someone else's life. It is not an account of someone else's success. It is a humble story of an ordinary person who rose from the bottom because I had enough of the unfair life, and I took the risks to fail and win in the end.

Chapter 1

Walking Through Darkness
Passing Through Pain

"We must embrace pain and burn it as fuel for our journey."

Kenji Miyazawa

We all experience pain and suffering in our lives. As human beings, we want to avoid it, get rid of it or even numb it. But we need to realize that God allows pain because our suffering is a sign of God's love.

Whenever we go through something big or small, pain is ever-present in our lives. It may be hard to accept but pain is an absolute necessity, thus, "Consider it pure joy, my brothers and sisters, whenever you face trials of many kinds, because you know that the testing of our faith produces perseverance. Perseverance must finish its work so that you may be mature and complete, not lacking anything." James 1:2-4

Pain.

Pain is one of those things that reminds us always that all human beings are equal. The young and the old suffer pain. The rich and the poor are visited by it. Neither the great nor the humble are spared pain. Pain is one experience that shouts to our ears how human, how vulnerable we are, how mortal we are, and how much in need of others we are. Pain, strangely, is one of those things that marks our humanity. When pain enters our lives, it has to be welcomed.

My past experiences truly shaped me well, so I never disregard my hardships. They prepared me mentally, physically, and emotionally to overcome the tough times in my journey. We must be willing to walk through darkness, for that's where the next morning awaits.

As a young child, I knew what I wanted. I wanted to break the chains of poverty my family had lived in for three generations. I was born the youngest of four children and grew up in a third world country in Asia, on the beautiful archipelago of the Philippines.

We hopped from one place to another because we couldn't pay the bills for our shack. Countless moves were made. There was no stability, and I hated it because people looked down on us. We were invisible from everyone. The biggest transition took place when my father moved us to his province, a small town in Mahanub, Surigao del Norte in Mindanao. It is the third major island group in the Philippines where most people lived a primitive life. The year was 1971.

We had been poor most of our lives, but our life hit rock bottom when my father lost his livelihood and everything he built, due to his careless accommodation and strong love for his brother. It turned out his brother used him for his own selfish desires. Our family suffered and experienced poverty. My father sacrificed and left his profession in the Philippine Air Force.

As we began our new and tough life in that small province, our family lived without electricity because it was in an underdeveloped and remote area. No TV, no refrigerator, no telephones, no lights except for kerosene lamps. People went to bed early because there was not much to do, especially when it gets dark early during the year. But we children learned to adapt after a year. We became appreciative of everything we had by living a primitive life. We found bliss in the streams where my siblings and I could dip ourselves in the water. We had great dogs, Jaguar and Whitey. We played with chickens and ducks. I watched my two older brothers, Edgar and Eman, ride "Kalabaws" (Carabao is a water buffalo). Some people walked barefooted. I remember watching my father's friends climbing up tall coconut trees, so fast, like monkeys. I was extremely fascinated. They were good people. Pure and kindhearted. When we visited their nipa huts, up in the hills, they would serve us boiled "nilagang camote" (sweet potato) and "nilagang saging" (banana plantain). I loved it.

When we woke up each morning, we could hear the birds chirping and the cock crowing. It was magical for me. To live in a "nipa hut" surrounded by tall coconut trees and the rain forest was quite an experience.

I played with fireflies, caught dragon flies, picked flowers, and played mostly outdoors. We took baths beside the deep well with my great grandmother "Uya" and the water was so cold. And oh, I remember, I had only one doll growing up and she was bald. I enjoyed making many dresses for her that I would sew by hand.

Looking back, I think it is so cool that I've experienced such a life. I wouldn't change that for anything. However, I don't know if I could survive that now that I have become dependent on all our technologies. We were still happy even with all those voids in our lives because love filled the air. I thank God for giving me the wisdom and understanding during my prime age to choose the positive views of life versus the negative because it allows me to appreciate and discover the meaning of life.

But I told myself that this has to change someday. Life at the bottom offers numerous challenges that lead to pain and loneliness, especially in times of turmoil like money issues to settle bills, acquire basic food, and necessities to survive. Often times, anxiety and depression visited me as a young child and led me to ask God, "Why are we stricken in poverty and are we going to get out of it?" It was not an easy life, you see.

After the second year, with no future lying ahead, the family moved back to Manila in Caloocan City. Since we didn't have any means, we found ourselves living in my grandparents' small apartment where we managed to squeeze our whole family, including us four children and my parents. My grandparents slept in another room with my aunt, her husband and two children.

Each morning, before my four mile walk to school, our mother, Rosa, would fix black coffee for us children and we would take two small rolls of bread, called "Pandesal" (hot round bread), break them into pieces, and dip them into our hot coffee. We got a taste of milk once a month. That is why I was thin and frail as I was growing up. We ate mostly fish and rice during lunch and dinner. If we were lucky, we might get a taste of meat once a month.

I learned how to sew my own dresses by remaking my mother's old clothes. I love sewing. I am very creative. I am an artist at heart. I love to sketch. I love to draw. My family and friends saw my talent. They enjoyed seeing my work from the time I was a little child all through high school. I always got an A+ in my art classes and dreamed of being a painter, but that dream got shelved because I couldn't afford the cost of attending a fine arts college.

Growing up, I loved watching cowboy and war movies on black and white TV with my father. I was very close to my father. I didn't see Walt Disney's *Cinderella* and *Snow White* because we could not afford to go to the movie theatres. I didn't see my first movie in a theater until I was in high school and saw *Grease* in 1978.

We never had vacations. The word "vacation" was not in my vocabulary until I reached the age of 34, when I was financially able to afford one. Crazy, isn't it? Despite all this, I considered myself a very happy child because our home was filled with Love.

You see, I missed out on a lot of things. Did I get mad? I was more sad than mad. I can't get mad for something that my parents can't afford to do. They were good parents. They would have given us everything in their power if they had the resources. So, I was sad. Sad that we did not have that ability to do things like others did. But one thing I know, and I always practice, is don't try to do things to compete with others if you can't afford to, because it may lead to harming you in the end. I believe in my heart that we will all take turns to shine in God's time. Our moment will come. And when it does, we need to embrace it with joy and thanksgiving. Let not jealousy nor enviousness enter your thoughts for I believe that jealousy does more harm to its owner than to its enemy.

The only thing I didn't like was the way the people around us often looked down on our family, most especially my parents, and that was very painful for me. That's when I began dreaming. I would ask myself, "What if? What if I bring prosperity to this family? What if I find a way to change our lives and create a lifestyle like others have?" My desire grew and grew, yet I lacked tools and resources because, clearly, I wasn't born with a silver spoon in my mouth.

I saw my siblings, my father and mother content settling for less of life. As I grew older, I told myself there's got to be a way out. There's got to be. I didn't know how, because I didn't have any resources, but I wasn't going to let that stop me. I would find an opportunity no matter what. Why did I constantly think these thoughts? Because my parents brought us back to Mindanao when I stepped into my first year in high school, but this time in Davao City. Again, no stability. No permanent address. It was difficult in every sense of the word.

I was a slow learner when I was a little child, but once I opened up my mind, it was like … Boom! By the time I reached high school, I started getting it. I would observe bright folks in class, how they spent their break time. Do you know what they did? They would play a dictionary game! They played something that entailed learning during the break-time? I thought they were crazy. No, they were brilliant. One person would look at the dictionary, pick a word, then give a hint to the other players. For example, the first person would begin by saying, "It's a nine-letter word that starts with the letter S and ends with the letter Y. 'An act of speaking one's thoughts aloud regardless of any hearers, especially a character in a play.' What is the word?" Whoever got the correct answer was the winner! Did you guess it? Soliloquy! Then the winner would take the dictionary and do the same thing.

Ugh! It drove me nuts. As I continued to observe these girls, I discovered the books they were reading, and I began reading them also.

Eventually, my mindset changed. I became one of the above-average kids, and I carried that through college. I achieved outstanding grades and was on the dean's list throughout college. To this day I value education.

I learned that by associating yourself with people who are winners, you will eventually become a winner, too. I learned who to follow in my younger years. I developed that kind of positive mentality. Competitive at all times, I hate missing out. I hate being last, and my family's status was the lowest back then.

I knew what I wanted, and I didn't want to continue the kind of life we were living. It was horrible in terms of how people treated our family. Always the underdog. Invisible! I asked myself, "Aren't all people valuable? Don't we all deserve respect?" That's been my point of view since day one.

I continued to enjoy life while looking for opportunities to live a better way. All I could think of was how to uplift the family, to escalate the family, to put my parents on a pedestal. No one else in the family was making an effort to improve our position. Nevertheless, poverty was not acceptable to me, so my search for the path to a better life continued.

My parents saw my ambition and my potential. With their help, I was able to graduate college. My mother exhausted her resources including what she made from her temporary part time job working in a manufacturing company in the assembly department. That work only lasted for a few months. My father, Cristino, only received meager Social Security income each month during that time, after he took a lump sum from his service in the Philippine Air Force. He also pushed himself to look for other means to earn extra income unfortunately, was unsuccessful.

By the time I reached college, my parents reached out to my sister and brother-in-law (who at that time were financially sound) to provide us a little assistance for my college expenses. However, the help didn't last and was discontinued after a year.

Grateful for every little blessing, I was able to give back to my sister and brother-in-law when they experienced hardships later on in life, when I reached success.

I dedicated myself to working harder because I wanted to give my parents a great lifestyle which they never had before. I thought it would be a priceless gift if they could experience it.

Achieving success in your career does not mean your personal life becomes perfect or easy. What people don't realize is that there are crippling anxieties and struggles along the way. As our life accelerates, we are also faced with massive adversities along the journey. That's life.

I was in my late twenties when I faced my first major loss. I lost my maternal grandmother, Josefa, whom I loved so much. It was very difficult for me when my grandmother died. I saw her as a saint, a martyr. Josefa was one of my heroes. She married a womanizer and she stayed with him until her death because she didn't want her children, my mother and my aunt, to have a broken family. But I didn't admire her for that. Instead, I admired her because of her love and dedication to her two children. She was a good and loving mother.

In 1974, I was only 11 years old when my family and I lived at our grandparent's place for a couple of years. That's when I established my relationship with my grandmother. She taught me how to fast (no food nor water) before going to church every Sunday. She told me that our bodies must be empty when we receive the Eucharist. She often took me to the wet market to buy our food. If she was lucky, she would get five pesos from my grandfather, who was feeding two families at that time. I loved going with her because she bought me my favorite delicacy called "kakanin," which is a sticky cassava cake.

My grandmother cooked my favorite Filipino food, like adobo and sinigang. Adobo is pork or chicken cooked in sauce, vinegar, laurel leaf, whole pepper and garlic. Sinigang is made up of pork ribs, with string beans, colocasia, tamarind sauce and water spinach.

I have fond memories of her. However, as a little girl I often wondered why Calixto, my grandfather, did not come home every day. It was years later before I learned that he had two families he was responsible for. Oftentimes, he did not give my grandmother the money to pay the rent. I would see my grandmother telling the landlord to come back week after week until the landlord would get mad at her. Thank God she paid her before we got evicted. That's where I learned true sacrifice.

My parents gave her meager help as much as they possibly could. My elder sister, Susan, and I would help Josefa make rugs, and we created sew-on snap buttons which we sold to a factory to make money. Josefa also raised and sold pigs. She would do anything to come up with money. We did a great job raising money for our food and rent while my father provided for our schooling, books, and clothing for four children.

My grandmother was a role model for me. I never once heard her complain. That's where I learned servant leadership. I was privileged to give back to her when I got older and took her and my parents under my wing. Unfortunately, she died at the age of 78 and I felt true pain, losing someone I love very much.

Darkness.

Another darkness followed when I became a single mother from my first marriage. I didn't see that coming. When I helped my ex-husband to get employment at the Shangri-La Hotel in Manila, I found out that he was having an affair with his female manager.

He almost missed out being in the hospital when I gave birth to our son, Nico, because his manager was giving him a hard time and not allowing him to miss work. It was insane. Because of this incident, I helped him get employment through a cruise line. Then again, I found out that he was having an affair with a married woman aboard the ship. Having three people in a relationship was too crowded for me and I made a choice. That was the last straw. I let him go and processed the annulment at my own expense, receiving no child support. Unfortunately, most men in the Philippines get away with not paying child support.

My parents were devastated. They were my emotional support system. At that time, I didn't know how to feel. I was numb. I developed anxiety and low self-esteem. I thought I had no worth and blamed myself. But the lion in me raised her head and I began to fight the lies I had told myself. I soon realized that he didn't deserve me. I deserved a better man. Being alone was a very good experience that has taught me how to love and appreciate myself. I took the time until my heart was ready to find love once again. It took me seven years to remarry again. I was cautious. I was afraid to fail in another marriage.

Because my life has not been an easy one, I know how you feel. In relationships, I know what it is to think you are not worthy to be loved, to lose someone you love, what it's like to do without. And in life, I loathe to be looked down upon, to struggle and to search for constant means to survive. But I am here to tell you, there is light on the other side of any darkness that comes into your life. I just happened to make the right preparation for my expedition – that is faith in God, belief in myself, and gratitude.

Aside from Jesus, my son Nico is the great instrument that God has given to me, that makes all challenges I face a triumphant journey. He saved my life from potential devastation.

After the break up of my first marriage, I focused my attention on my son. He was my inspiration. He gave me the strength I needed to get back up. It was challenging to be a single mother and the breadwinner of the family. My son was the source of my courage – courage I needed to walk through darkness hoping to see the light at the end of the tunnel. I was blessed to have my healthy child.

I was left into darkness, but I found light because I clung to God. When I did, I was guided to see the right people, say and do the right things, give the right kind of service and make myself valuable to others. Abundance to meet every good requirement was given to me. Favors from heaven came outpouring unexpectedly.

My life was difficult, and I had to sacrifice many things. I had to sacrifice being away from my son as I traveled globally to run my Asian telecommunications company. I had to sacrifice weekends with my friends so that I could spend time with my parents and son.

I even refrained from dating because my family was my top priority and being able to sustain our monthly financial expenses could not be overlooked. It took me five long years to finally find the love of my life, and another two years before I remarried again. That's how cautious I was in correcting my errors in the past. I was focused on giving my family a great lifestyle. I wasn't going to be content with just surviving; I was determined to create a lifestyle where we could all thrive.

I came out of that darkness of being a single mother. I left my life in the Philippines in 2003 to bravely embrace a new life of the unknown. At that time, I sold my company that had brought me from poverty to wealth. I left my life in Asia and brought my son with me to the United States when I married Greg, the man of my dreams. I chose LOVE, for where there is love, I believe wealth and success will follow.

He was the man I had prayed for, the man who God sent me, a truly good man who became a father to my son. He loved him like his own two children from his previous marriage. That was more than enough for me.

Another Darkness.

In 2004, my father died of an aneurism. That was the one of the most traumatic and darkest times of my life. I was in a state of shock when he was in the hospital in a coma. His vitals were low. Even if he woke up, the doctors said he would be a vegetable.

There was nothing I could do to help my father. It is unreal when you are not in control, but I acknowledged that my father's life was in God's hand. I wasn't ready to lose him at that time. It was a very painful moment. I was numb. It took me several years to begin recovering from his death.

My father was my best friend. He was my protector. He was my biggest fan. My supporter. My confidante. His love for me and my son was second to none. He made us both feel safe. He loved his entire family. He was my hero, a man of compassion and generosity, the life of the party. He was meek and humble, and brave. He was my lion. He was always there in every struggle I faced. He was the most sacrificial man I have ever met. He supported me as best he could with what he knew how to do. A true warrior, my father had a pure heart.

Material things didn't matter to him. What mattered to him was the heart of a person. Giving and loving, that's how I remember him. I grieved for five years after he died and cried each day. God took away one of my biggest loves, the person who stood by me and nurtured me like I was the most precious gem on earth. He appreciated all my hard work. That is very important and meaningful to me. He was so proud of me and all of my achievements. He made me feel loved. I am my father's shadow. I am my father. I am his protégé, and I miss that old man. Forever will I miss him, and I will continue to make him proud in heaven.

In life, winter normally represents periods of darkness. Years later another dark time occurred in my life. To some, winter can be long. But hush. You may not realize it until later, God will get you through all your adversities.

It was December 2014, with Christmas just around the corner, when my husband, Greg, and I faced the greatest obstacle in our lives. He was diagnosed with grade 3 brain cancer. Sadly, there was no cure for Anaplastic Astrocytoma. Greg was at very high risk of dying. My world was crushed. Again, I was numb. As he underwent surgery, radiation, and chemotherapy, I put a temporary halt to my global business. The medical doctors opted to give him a therapy that was not typically suited for grade 3 brain cancer, but there was no other option. Grade 4 therapy. No assurance of surviving.

More Darkness.

Was cancer really going to take away my husband? I was not ready to lose him. What would happen next?

Winters in our life will never be over. They will keep on coming back. We must stay vigilant. Our hearts must be strong. We must be ready. Afflictions and adversities come in our life like a thief in the night.

Six months into my husband's fight for his life, he got laid off from the company where he had worked for almost 19 years. They gave him two month's severance pay. I was ready to file a lawsuit against his company, but he didn't want to undergo such tedious times. He said, "We shall leave it up to God and pray. The most important thing right now is to survive and get rid of this cancer."

Every night, before bed, he would tell me, "I will get rid of this cancer, Kai."

Maybe he was just trying to make me feel good and stay strong and hopeful, but I saw the truth in his eyes. He was determined. No sadness in his face, but assurance in himself that he will get well by the Grace of God. We did not discuss any morbid subject like the will. All we did was spend time together each day praying a lot during his battle with brain cancer. It was hard to see him lose all his hair and lose 45 pounds. His breath smelled like metal. Chemo was toxic. I was scared.

Nico and Greg's other children, Grant and Michelle from his previous marriage, were devastated. They didn't know what to do and how to react. Family and friends prayed and lit candles during his battle with cancer.

Greg was absolutely broken as he hit rock bottom, but his faith in God was solid. He didn't complain once. He was ready to die if he was called by God, but he was determined he would survive it. I was the one who was not ready for him to die.

My global business I began building in the U.S. was put on hold for six months, and I thank God this business platform allowed me to be at my husband's side every single day during his battle with cancer. That's when I understood the power of "digging the well before getting thirsty." We are blessed to teach others do the same. When we educate each other, when we guide each other to reach success, we achieve the best of humanity.

By the grace of God, my husband is in his fifth year of remission. His latest MRI is favorable. Squeaky clean, he's cancer free!

And there is light after the darkness.

The next morning, after the darkness, feels victorious. It's glorious. The feeling is always glorious – like you have conquered many battles in life.

We face a lot of great battles, and the battles continue as we move through our life's journey. As we become victorious in these battles, another battle comes in, and we face it again. It is endless.

The darkness of winter is going to come every now and then. We can't change the seasons – winter, spring, summer or fall. We need instead to enjoy the seasons, because they bring us new life, new growth, new faith, new belief. It is exciting, because if we experience just summer, really, that's boring. There has got to be a winter, so there can be a hibernation time which will purify us so that we can get our strength once again.

The hibernation helps us to correct the errors of the past. "What have I done? What could I have done? What can I do better?"

The battles that we experience – are we going to just keep this inside? No. We need to share them with other people who are experiencing that battle now. One of the reasons I wrote this book is because I believe that a book is an opportunity to use our voice for the voiceless.

Maybe you are going through cancer. Maybe you are broken hearted. Maybe you are facing challenges with your children. Maybe your business is failing. We each experience battles in life. That's the reason why we are anointed. We are anointed by God to be an instrument to help other people, to bring them strength once again, to help others see the light and give hope.

Battles never end until we pass, until we are called home to God. Let's share the greatest battles that we have so that others can also face their battles with strength. This book is a call to action to become a lion at heart during our darkest times. We become one when we let the battle be God's.

Are we not all warriors? Yes, we are. We just have not yet unleashed the warrior within us because most people only use their intellect. There's something greater than intellect. It's our hearts. When our heart is wounded and we are facing massive obstacles, we need to rest in deep meditation. Give yourself time to discern what you desire to become. And when your heart is strong enough to depend on its inner strength, let it roar like a lion.

I surely do not wish that anyone should suffer pain of any kind. Much less would I want to inflict it with malice on anybody. But when pain comes, as sign of our humanity and as a signal warning us of our illusions, pain has to be welcomed.

I kindle such a hope that this book and my honest and humble words will help people. It's not about me. It's about being of value to others. It's about telling people there is light after darkness if you just remain in God's grip.

Lessons from the Lion's Heart

- Don't disregard hardships in life, for it will shape and prepare you well to achieve success.
- Darkness comes to everyone.
- Pain allows us to discover our inner strength.
- There is always light after darkness.
- Pain is a sign of our humanity, when it comes, pain has to be welcomed.

"The world is wounded. We are all patching holes in our life. As this world is wounded, we are all called to be shepherds. We are called to serve and inspire others and make a difference in someone else's life."

Kai Hayes

Chapter 2

Victories Over Sacrifices
There's No Victory without Sacrifices

"There are no secrets to success. It is the result of preparation, hard work, and learning from failure."

Colin Powell

Success requires some kind of sacrifice. We will not gain something for nothing. Our goals and objectives that we have in our minds will not magically manifest in our lives. We need to be willing to exert effort and work hard to make drastic sacrifices along the way. One must be willing to give up even to the point of putting aside their own personal dreams in order to serve others. The people in the world who achieve the most are the ones who are able to **sacrifice**.

My son, Nico, is my inspiration. He was a gift from the heavens. He brings out the best of the maternal in me. The joy he provides motivates me to go beyond breaking the chains of poverty in my family. Without my son I don't know where I would be.

When my son was about three years old, my marriage broke up. It was at that point that I took my son in my arms, with tears flowing down on my cheeks, and I whispered to him, "I promise you, my son, that I will do my best to make sure you won't have to grow up with the hardships and poverty that I did."

We all champion different causes. As for me, I saw a fight to provide my son a secure future. I dedicated myself to becoming a responsible mother. He is my best friend. We love, respect, and trust each other.

Truthfully, I didn't know what tomorrow would bring as the breadwinner for my family. All I knew was that I had a regular job that paid my bills and I had loving and supportive parents. In fact, I never complained about being the one who had to shoulder the major responsibility of providing for my family despite being the youngest of four children. Instead, I took it with no malice at all. Sadly, my three siblings got used to my support to the elders and treated it as my full obligation for 32 years, up to these present times.

My patience all throughout this incredible journey of the unknown is one of the greatest attributes I developed to attain victory. Had I not been patient, I would not have championed my cause. I worked long hours to provide my family the basic needs and pay my monthly bills.

Through the years, I developed a strong work ethic, which is one of the key ingredients of success. All I had in my mind was how to move forward and how to get ahead. I never looked back. I had one goal in mind: to WIN. Blessed with my inspiration, Nico, I did win. That is why I consistently achieved recognitions in past sales jobs, always achieving the top sales status. I was recognized as one of the consistent top producers, if not the top, at every company I worked for.

Early on, I understood that one must be willing to put forth massive effort consistently and commit oneself to grow, whether personal, spiritual or leadership growth. Preparation is the key.

I love what Jim Rohn, my favorite motivational speaker, teaches. He led an exemplary life as both an entrepreneur and an author. His eloquent speeches and unequivocal intellect brought him fame and glory as one of the most philosophical minds in all of America. He has inspired me to no end. He said, "The same wind blows on us all; the winds of disaster, opportunity and change. Therefore, it is not the blowing of the wind, but the setting of the sails that will determine our direction in life."

However, not a lot of people are willing to do what it takes to become successful. Everybody, one hundred percent everybody, wants to be successful. The greatest challenge to success is willingness to embrace discipline. Are you willing to commit 100 percent? And when you commit, are you willing to be consistent with what you have committed?

Success is a process. I invest in myself. I see to it that I represent every company I work for, as well as my current global business, with integrity. I believe in giving genuine outstanding after-sales service. Outstanding customer service is the new sales. That is one ingredient of my success. Even though I competed with many others, in the end I was always the top salesperson because I had my customers' loyalty.

Don't doubt yourself by comparing yourself with other people's attributes and assets. You can leverage your own outstanding qualities and use them for good.

Success equals sacrifice and sacrifice equals success. Are you willing to persevere? The road ahead will have a lot of obstacles.

In fact, we have no idea where we are going because we do not see the road ahead. We cannot know for sure where it will end – in victory or in failure.

Never think that victory is easy to achieve. Many famous, successful figures achieved victory only after massive failures. The only difference is that they never gave up. I think I have those characteristics. Quitting is never entertained in my mind. I could have settled for a mediocre life, but I have a burning desire in my heart that I too can do what other successful individuals do and have what they have.

It sounds superficial, and I might make it sound easy. Well, allow me to share with you the tough life I had working my way up the corporate ladder. It was a constant, horrible struggle.

First, in my sales endeavors I had to meet my quota each month. But I was not content with just meeting my quota. I was focused on improving my life. So, I trained my mind not to settle for less. I not only met my monthly quota for years, but I doubled and tripled my output in every sales job I had. Yes, I've always been an asset to every company I worked for.

My success didn't come easily like others might think. When I embarked on my journey in the banking arena, I had to put my best foot forward to excel. When I transitioned to building my global business in the latter years, numerous times I would sleep in many different houses, different time zones, sometimes at different hotels. I endured long layovers at the airport. The longest I had was 12 hours. I slept at the airport. I traveled alone while I was building my team. I had to stay away from home for days, even weeks as needed. I did what was needed and required for me to do. I had no other options.

Everyone must remember this:

"When we look at some of the world's greatest advancements and innovations, and some of our planet's most brilliant scientists, researchers and leaders, we often bask in the glow of their positive outcomes. But what we don't see is everything that happened between start to finish. We don't see the crippling anxiety and the massive failures and the terrible missteps."

— Ry Fry

Never take your hardships for granted. Are you getting impatient because it seems nothing is going to change? Are you working hard but you feel like you are in the hamster wheel, doing the same thing over and over?

I was willing to take any risk. I am not afraid to look for other resources, look for another avenue for success.

By all means prepare. Preparation is the key to success. The best preparation for tomorrow is doing your best today.

Until you find a good reason to fight for something, fight for your own cause, you will not be able to find the strength you need to achieve a victorious battle.

In my case, I was fighting for my son, my parents and grandparents. I was fighting to get out of poverty. I was fighting for myself, too. These were great causes.

I could have taken the easy way out. When I was younger, I was pursued by many successful men. I could have recklessly jumped into another marriage and lived a comfortable life. You know, marriage for convenience? But those thoughts were not entertained by me at all. Why? I want to bring honor to my family.

Most of all, I want my son to look up to me and be proud that his mother chose to work hard rather than to marry for convenience. There is nothing wrong if other people choose the latter reason. I respect people's choices and their beliefs. We all have our unique journey, so who am I to say my direction is the right path?

Our life is full of stumbling blocks. We are the ones who will fix our own mess. Each person has their own choices and views. I am just telling you what my views are. If you find great value to my choices and actions, then own it.

So instead of marrying for money, I searched for a full-time job and later embraced sales. Sales allowed me to earn more than the average salary and I needed extra income to pay all the bills. I had rented a small place and took my parents and grandparents to live with me.

Sacrifice. Sacrifice comes before success or victory. Ask yourself, are you truly willing to embrace **sacrifice** as much as you want **victory**?

Let me share with you another success journey I had as I continue my life here in the United States. I left my successful life in Asia in 2003 when I married my soul mate, Greg. It was a challenging decision because I was at the height of my success. How many people would sacrifice wealth for love?

I sought discernment through deep meditation and prayers. I did not second guess my decision. I chose love. I will always choose love, for where there is love, success and wealth will follow.

Did I see it right away? No. I had no clue that success and wealth would follow right away. I was content with finding true love. I appreciate every blessing that comes my way.

I sold my international telecommunications business and migrated to the United States with my son. Sadly, I left my parents, my three siblings, and their families. By that time my grandparents had already passed away.

My son and I started our new life. While I had a good chunk of proceeds from the sale of my company, it got depleted after five years of being a stay-at-home mom. However, I had set aside funds for my son's college so he would never have to worry about college loans.

My husband was the sole breadwinner and after five years of being a stay-at-home mom, I got bored and went back to work as a business banker. By that time, I was not wired to be an employee anymore and felt like I wasn't getting paid my worth. I wasn't in control. I was building someone else's dreams.

In spite of the success I achieved in just 18 months as one of the top business bankers in the entire Austin, Texas district, I wasn't happy. I worked at the bank for only three years and began searching for a better way.

My prayers were answered. While working at the bank I discovered a powerful business platform, it was a whole new, unique idea for me. I've always had traditional jobs and worked in traditional businesses. But given my tough life in the past, I learned to have an open mind. The platform I discovered was network marketing, where I learned how to create leveraged income.

I was smart enough to investigate and educate myself about this industry. When I fully understood the business concept, it changed my perspective. I love learning new things, especially if the idea is brilliant and something that works 100 percent.

I fell in love with the business model. I took it seriously, learned it, and ran with it. I established my leveraged income after four years. Victory took place. It was a gift. My world changed forever.

I also became the leader that I dreamed of, which enables me to serve humanity. I get to transfer my belief, my heart and my all to individuals who are seeking inspiration to better their life.

As a result, I was able to conquer one of my greatest fears — talking in front of a large group of people. This didn't happen overnight. It took years to develop my confidence. My biggest moment came when I was given the opportunity to speak in front of thousands of people seeking inspiration and courage.

I wasn't profound, but I spoke from my heart. That's when I realized being me and pouring out the love in my heart was more than enough for people to trust and respect me. It was a glorious time.

I continued with my journey and worked for another four years to double my leveraged income. On the ninth year building my global business, my husband was able to quit his corporate job on his 60th birthday last November 2019 after 37 years he spent in the workforce.

Favors from God outpoured. My husband and I are grateful. In addition, we built our dream home in October of 2019. We could not ask for more. Our health is outstanding. Thanks be to God.

Were all of these victories easy? Not at all. Countless candles were burned, meaning I worked long hours and mostly away from home. Behind victory is massive sacrifice and proper preparation.

In this current and tough economy, not a lot of people can go in that direction. Most people are looking to add second jobs and can't retire.

Will you wait until catastrophe happens in your life? Or will you stay vigilant and learn how to sacrifice? Keep an open mind. Open your door to every opportunity. Scrutinize ideas. Make sure you ask a lot of questions that could lead to a sound decision. Watch where most people are going and make sure you get there first.

Ask yourself. Are you willing to spend long hours, days, or weeks away from your spouse and family? Can you accept that there will be short-term imbalance for a long-term victory? Are you willing to give up some things that may seem highly important to you and your family now, while you are on a special journey?

The biggest problem in this arena is that many people, more often than not, are not willing to give up the things that are insignificant in their lives. They spend too much time with the things that don't help them grow. Sadly, most people want to have quick gratification.

Are you willing to embrace loneliness in your tough journey? One must be willing to be independent and able to work alone when necessary.

My remarkable journey in building a global business was mostly spent alone in the beginning. My husband attempted to kick start this new career with me, but we realized one of us had to fuel our daily needs and pay our bills, while the other learned the necessary skills to be successful. He and I made an agreement. He would work full time while I built my global business.

I would not allow myself to fail. I would not fail my husband. I would not fail my family. This unique business model was a gift from God. I knew I must act upon it and not take God's gift for granted. That's how I think. When I discern God's gift, I will put my best effort forward, and I'll give it back ten-fold if I can.

Never forget, sometimes we all have to go through some things in our life alone. Remember that loneliness has a way of making us learn how to trust and believe in ourselves, and to depend on our inner strength and courage until our heart becomes stronger.

If you wish to follow successful people and achieve what they have achieved, you must be willing to sacrifice things that are tough to give up. Are you willing to break through regardless of your current circumstances? If you are, then you are ready!

People complain about the old system, but they are not willing to embrace a new way. They say they're "sick and tired of being sick and tired," doing the same things over and over. Unfortunately, those individuals are the ones who are close-minded and are not willing to educate themselves with new ideas. That's the definition of insanity. Have a positive mind set and explore new avenues that could lead to what you are searching for.

Many people make excuses. No matter which path in life or business you choose, it takes sacrifice to achieve success. You must be willing to be uncomfortable and be willing to get out of your comfort zone. When you do, that's when miracles happen.

I worked hard to get out of my comfort zone. Would you believe that it took me a year to find courage to speak in front of 10–12 people? I love talking to people one on one, but not in front of an audience. It's really nerve-wracking to learn how to speak in front of the public. I bet some of you who are reading this book feel the same way! However, I am willing to learn. I am coachable. Are you?

I am always fascinated with the great speakers I watch on stage like Robert Kiyosaki, Erin Brokovich, John Maxwell, and Eric Worre, to name a few. I dreamed of becoming a speaker, but I was petrified each time I thought of doing it. Through years of practice I find myself speaking in front of thousands of people. It is unreal. I have conquered fear victoriously.

Now that I have achieved success in my current industry, I am summoned to speak at various events and conventions, and to small groups of people. I will never say no to opportunities. That's who I am. I was determined to embrace change – change for the better, not for the worse.

I understood instinctively that if I wanted my family's status to change, I needed to change. I refused to follow my siblings' route. I love and respect them, but they have a different mindset. It is more than enough for me to show them my exemplary work with the hope of inspiring them.

Again, it is a matter of choice. A servant mindset is essential. The only thing in my mind was how to put my family on a pedestal. How could I bring respect to my family? Making a success of myself was the only answer.

Looking back, it is sad that my parents didn't champion their causes. Perhaps they did, but they didn't win. I was determined to win for them and when I did, people began to look up to them. It was fulfilling when neighbors, friends and relatives developed respect towards us.

In order to live a successful life, we must seek to achieve time, health, and financial freedom. If you can achieve all three, then you are invincible. However, no one is perfect. We just try our best and that is enough.

Sacrifice-wise, I was head on. I knew it was not going to be easy to achieve greater success than anyone in my family had before me. Nothing is easy and we need to accept that. Whatever you're doing, you better be committed 100%, and you must do things consistently because if you fail to be consistent then that's the beginning of a fall. Be consistent or you will fail.

When I was struggling to work my way up, even while I was still in the Philippines, I refrained from going out with my friends very often. I don't drink. I don't smoke. I never tried drugs. I was just not into it. I love clothes and shoes, though.

My friends would tease me because I was always the first to go home early. I would excuse myself to go to the powder room, but I didn't go back, ha! My weekend was normally spent with my son, his cousins, and my parents. I would take them for weekend vacations, making up for the years I never had one.

I developed discipline. That discipline, I took to my work world, my job. That's why I became very successful in whatever jobs I had.

Becoming a lion at heart is not for the faint of heart. One must be willing to take massive risks, for it requires sacrifice, persuasiveness, tenacity, commitment, and discipline. Heart is not something you can give someone. It's something that gets transformed within them.

I came from rock bottom and I transformed those experiences to develop a lion's heart. You too can develop a lion's heart, but it takes time to acquire that quality. The lion's heart is yours if you are willing to face adversities, seek and hunt for success, and are not willing to settle for less. Then, there is hope.

More victory.

In the U.S., when I was privileged to take the stage and speak about the topic of breaking through barriers, I brought all of my mentors who were a part of my success up onto the stage with me and expressed my gratitude to them in front of thousands of people. Humility and meekness are the way I desire to conduct myself. For no one can boast of our own achievements compared to God's standards. It was my main message to all. My spirit was lifted up. All I know is I represent God and He is pleased.

That is what matters most to me. To give hope. To touch people's lives. To come together and help champion causes for others. To bring out the lion in everyone's heart. When I am given the opportunity to speak, I don't take it lightly. I want to be compelling. I want people to remember me and my message. I want to inspire them. I want to bring tears or laughter in their hearts. When we are compelling, we are remembered forever.

That's the inner lion in me, willing to serve and also willing to fight. We know that lions will fight when need be. They don't pick fights, but because they are willing to protect their food, their mates, their territory and so forth, they will fight if necessary. What is the one thing you are willing to fight for?

You've got to be willing to pay a price, because success doesn't come without it.

Success has a story to be told. Success has a compelling story. All of the success in a person's life has a moving story.

The best thing is to inspire other people with your positive behavior. Share your story, your sacrifices behind your success. Inspire.

Speak from the heart and share those sacrifices. Your experience is what allows you to take your life to the next level. That is what people would love to hear right now.

I want to represent the masses. I want to be the voice for the voiceless. I feel their pain. I want to speak for the lowly, for the wounded. I want to speak for the people who are in pain or suffering, who are feeling like they're inadequate, the ones who hate themselves, the ones who experienced darkness in life, who don't have anything or have lost everything. The underdog. I want to represent them because I was once there.

I was once like you. I was one of you who are reading this book.

Lessons from a Lion's Heart

- To achieve victory, find a good reason to fight for something.
- Be willing to serve and not to be served. There's no victory without sacrifice.

- Preparation is the key to victory.
- The best preparation for tomorrow is doing your best today.
- Success is a process. Perseverance and commitment are needed.

"Be willing to go through our lives alone and depend on our inner strength and courage. And when our heart is strong enough, we become a LION AT HEART."

Kai Hayes

Chapter 3

Mission and Vision
Creating a Road Map for Success

"A spirit with a vision is a dream with a mission."

Neil Peart

E verybody needs to have a plan. Even the engineers need to have a blueprint because the blueprint provides a proven strategy that works for everyone to follow.

Continue to focus on your goals. If any activity does not support your goals, avoid it.

We can create our own blueprint for our future. Companies have to develop plans to follow in order to be successful. My current global company even calls its corporate plan/system a blueprint that all our field distributors must follow should they wish to create a successful global business.

Every business has competition and a good leader should be assertive, energetic and have a plan in place to implement the changes necessary to deal with that competition. When the team is overworked, good leaders know how to delegate the work amongst their team or are willing to add resources to complete the tasks if needed.

It's always the structure and the roadmap that can potentially lead everyone to success, which is followed by, of course, ambition, discipline and willingness to sacrifice.

First let's define a mission. A **mission** represents your objectives. Objectives are what you do in order to achieve your vision.

Vision is, basically, your ultimate goal. What you want to accomplish. Mission is the how. Vision is the why.

Maybe finishing college is first for you. What's your next plan? Will you become a manager or director? What's your next quest?

I wanted to land a good job after college. I started my first job as a receptionist in a computer school in Manila, where I began my quest for success.

After my grandparents lost their place, my parents, grandparents and I had to live with my married sister temporarily. My two other brothers, at this point, were living with their significant others. After about three years, when I was 25 years old, I had no choice but to take my family out of my brother-in-law's home. They could no longer accommodate our long stay. My father and I overheard my sister and her husband's conversation, telling her to kick us out of their home. My brother-in-law told my sister, "Tell them to move out or I will throw their personal belongings out of the window." These painful words never left me and became embedded in my brain. I told myself, "It doesn't have to be this way." I took the words literally and seriously. My heart was crushed. My parents and I had no place to stay and I was not making enough money as a receptionist. I put urgency into this matter and started searching for a higher paying job opportunity.

I found a better job and became a personal secretary to the famous landscape architect IP Santos. Santos was a Filipino architect known for being the *Father of Philippine Landscape Architecture*. He was recognized as a National Artist of the Philippines in the field of Architecture in 2006.

From there, I went on to become the executive assistant to the famous Cora Doloroso, the founder of First Major School of Fashion in Manila, at the Cora Doloroso Career Centre, where I also taught personality development and became her co-executive producer in Cora Doloroso fashion shows held at several five-star hotels in Manila.

Next, I landed in a Taiwanese modelling agency based in Manila, where I became a commercial and print ad model. I had several exciting experiences during my prime age when I was single. This is when my family would see me in TV commercials. I would bring home a magazine where I was featured in print ads. It was fun during the commercial shoots, especially when I got a handsome partner in the ads with me ha! I met so many friends and talent scouts who gave me more offers. But with so many models competing for the same commercial roles, I couldn't expect to get all the projects necessary to establish a steady income. As much as I loved modeling, the pay was not sufficient to be able to support a family of five. The search continued.

Then, I worked at a Mitsubishi car dealer as an encoder but was not equipped with typing abilities. They moved me to the sales department where I excelled after being trained for only three months. I had no experience in sales, but I was willing to learn. Being in sales shifted my attitude because then I began to observe the successful salespeople. My life began to change. I sought guidance and wisdom from them. I took the advice of the good ones and ignored the advice of the not so good ones. This is the first victory I won to support my parents and grandparents!

We moved out of my sister and brother-in-law's home. I rented a place in the same city, and I asked my best friend, Olive, to live with us. Her rent contribution helped sustain me while I was figuring out how to earn more. Remember, this was my first time to shoulder a huge responsibility. Paying the rent, utility bills, putting food on the table, and much more. I didn't have my own car yet. I commuted to work every day on the bus, and oh when it was typhoon and flood season, Olive and I would get soaked, in spite of having umbrellas. It took two to three hours to get home because the traffic was massive.

My ambition didn't stop there. I moved to Toyota car dealership where the compensation was more lucrative. Again, I became the top salesperson in less than a year. I bought my first car, a used 1995 silver Toyota Corolla. Things accelerated a bit on my end. Nothing great, but I was able to provide for my family.

I admit I was money-driven because I needed to sustain myself and my family. I worked hard and did not take time to play, but I never complained. I enjoyed the journey even though I worked long hours.

As I became successful, I received many offers from other companies. I landed in the telecommunications company called Extelcom. This was when the Micro-Tac phone became mainstream in the Philippines. At this point, I was married to my first husband. I was making enough commissions to shoulder everything and support my parents' and grandparents' needs. My husband did not earn as much as I did, but his salary helped.

I was inspired by the company's top salesperson, Katz Llamas. I admired her from day one. I wanted to be like her. And so, I did become like her. I achieved the top sales position in just six months. It was a healthy competition. We were both confident about ourselves. We were never jealous of each other. That's pure professionalism. I love that kind of mentality. We are still friends.

When my first marriage failed when I was 33 years old, I did not have a chance to grieve so much because I had a family to provide for. There was no time to waste and the clock was constantly ticking. My mission and vision grew stronger. I told myself, "My life has to improve every few years, if not each year." I was hungry. That burning desire grew each day. No one can teach you that. Not your husband, not your children. It must be coming from your heart.

While I worked in sales, I focused on learning skills and picking the brains of the brilliant executives I met as I handled the accounts of the top 1000 corporations in Manila. I forged strong relationships with key decision makers by earning their respect and providing excellence in customer service.

After working for Extelcom, I got a better opportunity and joined Enclosures System Inc., an international reseller company for Rittal Ltd., headquartered in Germany. That job required me to travel to Singapore and Germany, the first two international countries I visited. Traveling was an eye-opener, a life changing experience. I had never travelled outside of the Philippines in my life. I excelled in this company as well, but I never got a raise in two years, in spite of my outstanding performance. I was their top sales manager. Thus, my quest continued.

I was not afraid to hop from one company to another. As much as I wanted to stay in one company to attain stability and growth, I had a family to feed. At that time, my focus was to earn more than enough money to pay my bills, put food on the table for my dependents, and raise our status to the next level. I became the lioness whose job is to hunt for food. I also become the male lion, because I was looking to accelerate our lives to protect us from being treated so poorly by the upper classes. At that point, I didn't realize I was developing so much courage. I was not afraid to take any risks and learn new skills. If the company was not paying me my worth, I would leave and look for another that valued me better.

These experiences have shaped me well. I am thankful and grateful to God. I developed strong work ethics. I found a good reason to wake up each morning because I was providing a good life for my family. I became an asset to each company I worked with. I never doubted my worth because I over-deliver; I over-perform.

At age 35, I became highly recruited by other companies based on my strong performance and quality service in sales. In the process, I accepted a lucrative offer as a sales and marketing director for a U.K. based telecommunications company, GNComtext Ltd. I began to see more European countries as I traveled for trainings, conventions, and annual meetings. Recognitions followed me very quickly. It was fulfilling and I made my family proud. I excelled once again. This is when I improved our life status in the community. God's favor was with me.

However, when GNComtext Ltd. was later acquired by Easylink Services Inc., a U.S. company based in New York, my position became redundant and they offered me a good severance package. When I lost my position, I panicked as I was unlikely to get another job like that, which had accelerated my financial status. My dreams were shattered.

But alas, after a few months, I received a new opportunity from my former boss who had been rehired by Easylink Services. Thank God I was a strong performer, and had proven myself valuable to the company.

In 2000, I joined Easylink Services in a new role which gave me a life changing opportunity. This time as an independent business owner. I signed an exclusive contract as an international reseller company in Asia. I had never owned a company, and I didn't know how to run a business. Wow! It was too good to be true, a once in a lifetime opportunity, especially in a third world country. I was in shock.

On top of that, Easylink Services provided a huge acceptance package with my new company, World Premier Telecoms Inc. Everything I needed to kick-start my business was provided. I rented a plush office in a plush commercial location – Ayala, Alabang, an upscale location where the wealthy reside.

I bought a nice home. I bought two cars, one for me and one for my father. I hired three stay-in helpers – one for me, one for the household so my parents need not do chores, and one for my son. It was day and night – from rags to riches. It was overwhelming. My friends and relatives saw the transition. Things began to change around us.

As I reached success, I began my ministry of helping and serving others outside of my family. I established the Bridge of Hope Ministry, helping impoverished children in the Philippines. My family and I visited slum areas and provided used clothes, books, school supplies, toys and bags of food. I partnered with St. Rita Orphanage where we send funds to supply food, clothes, and medical supplies for orphans. In addition, I am currently sponsoring a seminarian to priesthood at the Diocese of Tanzania and supporting St. Rita Catholic nuns to travel and attend retreats.

I continue to learn and develop bravery. Specifically:

- Bravery to discover what really makes me happy (my family)

- Bravery to ignore what others think is successful and find my own success (celebrate my own success)
- Bravery to make constant and dramatic changes to my career path that will also change my personal life. (This is my quest.)

We all champion different causes. Fight for what you believe is pure. Work hard for what you are fighting for. I say unto you, *"When you achieve your vision, mark your freedom, for God did not create people to own people."*

I clung to God even more then as my world began to change. This is when my faith grew deeper as this was true Grace. A great favor. It was a miracle. God saw my determination. My Sacrifice. My dedication to my elders. It was also a huge responsibility. However, I never thought of failing. As a single mother and breadwinner, Jesus poured mercy upon me, upon my great cause. I gave the glory to God and used this company for good. It was an incredible journey.

What is your cause? Don't be afraid to step out of your comfort zone. Tighten your grip on Jesus. He will walk with you, so allow Him to fight your battles when it gets tough.

My friends were astounded. My detractors tried to pull me down out of jealousy. Enemies tried to break me and concocted lies to hurt my reputation to try to transfer and steal this exclusive agreement with the principal to them. But I tell you now, no one can put a good woman or a man down. Because the truth will always prevail. They were unsuccessful with their bad intentions. Victory was mine. Have you ever had someone in your life like that? People who can't be happy for other people? Learn how to detach yourself from those type of people. They only bring ill things in your life.

I hired the right people – receptionist, administrative manager, tech guys, accountant, and salespeople – and created a winning team. We had unbeatable sales performance and continued to get paid our share as an exclusive reseller in Asia.

I continued this remarkable journey. I experienced many new things, yet I remained the same person who grew up in poverty. I shared my blessings with my siblings and their children.

I traveled a lot in various countries, sacrificing my time at home. I had to be away from my son, but I knew how to make up for my lost time with him. He was my top priority. To share my blessings, I would take all my family, including my siblings and their families, to theme parks, upscale restaurants and malls, vacation resorts, and many other exciting places.

As I saw more of the world, I was more humbled by it. I wasn't worthy of all these massive changes in my life. It was indeed just one great favor from God. I was rewarded for my strong work ethics, commitment, and dedication to achieve my vision. I continued traveling and exploring the world, seeing places I had never seen before. Meeting highly educated people without fear, sitting down having meetings with top international executives.

As one of the numerous international resellers worldwide, I was the only woman sitting in a conference room for annual meetings other than the secretary during that time. With various gentlemen around, it gave me a kick that I could freely speak my mind, without my words being taken personally. That's when I developed a better understanding how to best present myself as a respectable woman in a man's world. Firm and straight to the point. I conquered my fears.

My hard work paid off. That's the name of the game. Have you ever experienced it in your life? Where your hard work truly paid off? Not only hard work but honest work. Always give your best performance and deliver challenging tasks in a timely manner. Don't settle for less. Get to the top.

My advice is work honestly. Be worthy so you can find a worthy job. And when detractors come into your life, no one can win against you. Because no one can put a good person down. When you are with God, who can be against you, right?

Decide what your mission is. Remember, your mission is the "how." What do you want to do? When you figure out your mission, chances are you will be able to figure out your vision. Your vision is your "why." Your why is your ultimate goal and what you want to accomplish.

As for me, my mission in my current profession is to do the best I can to develop the skills I need to be competitive and to help others achieve success. I want to learn and apply the right skills in order to see my vision. There is no doubt about my mission, it's non-negotiable.

But how? How do I execute my mission? Well, I have to have the vision in order to fulfill my mission, right? So, my why – or vision – is to see myself accelerate and continue to create a good lifestyle and future for my family. Also, to reach financial freedom, maintain good health, and help others achieve their mission in life.

You have to make a decision about which direction you want to head. Establish a road map. What do you want to do? It's not about what is available. What do you want to do that makes you happy or fulfilled? Because you know what? If you don't like your job, then that quest is absolutely not going to happen.

However, it might take time to find what you like to do in life. So, explore out in the far horizon until you find what you are looking for! Ask yourself, with your mission and vision, who is involved? Is it just about you or does it involve someone else? Is helping others a part of your vision?

When you figure out your quest, make sure you focus and set aside a sacred time for your cause. Don't give up too easily. *When there's no pain, there's no glory.*

Conquer what you have to conquer. Even the Kings and Queens, they want to conquer territories. They have a quest; they have a plan because they want to rule and become the most powerful country in the world. They don't give up easily. They will fight until they have exhausted their resources. And when they reach the end of their resources, they will come up with other ideas or options to win the battle. They are conquerors! We all must be conquerors, in a good way and for a good cause.

The number one thing that I would like to share is, find your **purpose**. What do you like to do? What are you passionate about? If you are doing something you are passionate about, you will be more successful because you can stay the course. If you don't like what you're doing, chances are you're going to quit.

For example: who likes banking? I did. I really wanted to experience becoming a banker. So I did, when we moved Austin, Texas in 2008. They have a system that I had to learn and I was not computer savvy like the Gen-Xers. The training was grueling for me. I didn't like it, but I was determined to finish it. I stayed behind after class each day to complete my tasks. Deployment took place after 90 days in training. All 27 newly hired business bankers, including myself, were assigned to various bank locations in Texas. Six months after probation only three of us remained; the others were fired for non-performance.

In life, sometimes we unfortunately meet people who makes our life miserable without a cause. The branch manager I was assigned to during my training period was not a good person. He put me in a teller position for a long time. It wasn't what I applied for and worse yet, he assigned me to work on weekends. And lastly, he didn't allow me to travel with my family for our summer vacation that we booked a year before. He said, "I have a bank to run, I want you to show up at work or you will get fired." We cancelled our vacation and it cost us $600 dollars for the cancellation fee. Was that harsh or what?

Simply, he had no heart. I found out from other bank tellers that they could take their vacation and catch up with the training when they got back. I experienced cruelty from the manager. He didn't know what I had achieved before in my past careers. But did I treat him the way he treated me? No. I passed the training and I worked productively until I was put on a pedestal. I received massive recognition and a promotion. I then requested to be transferred to another branch and the manager who treated me badly lost my outstanding sales to the other bank where I transferred. Don't let obstacles get in your way. Fight a good fight to win in a positive way.

It was hard, but with discipline I became the top banker in the whole district of Texas within 18 months. It was a blessing, but I only worked for that company for three years. I didn't want to be working for someone else's dreams anymore.

By the grace of God, I discovered the right business opportunity that offered a solid platform that helped me achieve my true vision in life. That became my mission.

Having a plan is important to understand. Nobody can become rich overnight unless they are doing illegal things, or unless they win the lottery. There is no honor in that.

I am a very sensitive person, but I am strong when I need to be. Do I get scared? Yes. I am scared of the unknown. That is why I prepare. I stick with my mission and execute the right actions to achieve my vision.

Who would think that at this point in time, while I am writing this book, that the world would be affected by this COVID-19 pandemic in 2020? Unfortunately, millions of people have been infected and hundreds of thousands of people have died globally, especially those whose health was unstable. Many businesses have closed, as have major events, restaurants and shopping malls. Flights are limited. Millions of people have filed for unemployment.

Had I not chosen a business model that can sustain us during the times of crisis like this, I probably would not be able to enjoy the liberty of writing this book.

Lessons from a Lion's Heart

- Go for an expedition. Discover things as you are experiencing life.

- Decide the career and personal path you are going to follow based on what you are passionate about.

- Consider options that never occurred to you before.

- Be willing to commit and stay consistent to what you are envisioning.

- Give it a chance. Don't give up at the first difficulty.

"When you achieve your vision, mark your freedom, for God did not create people to own people."

Kai Hayes

Chapter 4

Pursuit of Greatness
Pursuing Makes a Difference

"Never underestimate the power of dreams and the influence of the human spirit. We are all the same in this notion: The potential for greatness lives within each of us."

Wilma Rudolph

There are a lot of great leaders who inspire me to the core of my being and that's the reason why I follow them. I want to make my own greatness. "We are all called to do great things, yet in order to do so we must find a way to serve the many, for serving the many leads to greatness." That's according to one of my favorite mentors, Jim Rohn.

With my current global business platform, I am able to help and serve others better. I can help them improve their health and wellness. I can help them achieve financial freedom. I can help them become the leaders they want to be. This platform allows individuals to discover and achieve personal growth, spiritual growth and outstanding leadership. It is life changing.

But you cannot achieve greatness right away. You need to take one step at a time, one step, one step, one step.

Lao Tzu says, "The journey of a thousand miles begins with one step." Move forward just one day at a time, and accomplish little things, and little things can be good things.

We all need to understand that anyone, even an ordinary person can achieve greatness. Ordinary people can do extraordinary things.

Get rid of the things that do not add value to your life, whether it's friends, family, peers, acquaintances, or thoughts that do not serve your goals.

Think good thoughts. I began thinking good thoughts because we need to be careful what we think since our thoughts can become things, which in time become habits.

Our lives are filled with numerous personal crossroads, moments when we are summoned to make a decision. With careful mental preparation, we can make wise choices. New disciplines must be practiced daily with the potential of producing exciting results.

Instill in your heart and mind the things that you can do to make a positive difference in your life and other people's lives. Don't focus on what you don't have; focus your attention on the things that you could potentially have, then give your best to make it happen.

Neglect is often the major reason why people don't have what they want. If we do not practice taking care of things in our lives, neglect becomes a disease. If we neglect our health or our finances, we certainly could be at risk. Begin setting up new and positive behaviors and practices that can lead to a better life.

Persevere to make it happen. Achieve great things one step at a time.

Some of your projects will pan out, some won't. Who cares? Look for another project after you have exhausted yourself and truly concluded it is not the right direction for you.

Observe and listen.

Pay attention during your day. Watch what's going on. Surround yourself with people you respect and admire. People whose achievements stimulate, fascinate and inspire you. Seek sound advice from good mentors. Be a good listener. Don't do things alone. Don't be afraid to reach out for help, but find a voice that could be of value in your life. Be cautious about whose advice you take.

We've got to focus our thoughts on goodness, abundance, and prosperity. It's the law of attraction. If you are really serious about achieving greatness, well, you must be willing to do the things that ordinary people won't do.

People, including my friends and peers, would try to figure out why and how I have achieved the successes that allowed me to accelerate my status. Most say I was just born hardworking. I was born a go-getter. I am an extrovert. I am a people person. I am great in sales. I am very charismatic. The truth is, I am not any of those.

I was a shy little girl. My mother would attest to this statement. I was a very quiet girl, the baby in the family. I was an introvert. I was afraid of people, especially in a crowd. I have low self-esteem. I didn't have a clue how to become the breadwinner of the family at a young age. I just did it when I knew I needed to.

When I did, all I focused on was how I could do things right. I couldn't afford to fail and disappoint my parents and grandparents.

No one was going to help them. I asked myself over and over again, "How can I excel? How can I bring glory to this family? How can I bring pride back to our name?"

Greatness comes from the desire to do extraordinary things – to try and reach beyond the status quo, to relentlessly chase your dreams. It all starts with setting and achieving goals, and when you aim higher than where you set your mark, you will force yourself to get better, one victory at a time, one step at a time.

We don't measure greatness with other people's achievements. Individuals can achieve greatness in a very special way. Be happy with your own greatness, big or little, as long as you impact people's lives. That is considered greatness.

Little things can make an impact through our own simple greatness, so it's not always easy to measure. The most important thing is how many people you have inspired and touched and motivated, and the people you have helped and served.

You achieve your own greatness in a way that you are capable.

Sometimes I still feel inadequate, and my husband tells me, "Are you kidding me? Who does what you've done? Who does what you did? You have provided for your parents. You've helped your grandparents. You've helped your three siblings. By taking all the responsibilities without your other siblings' help is helping them as well. You took away their responsibility as the other children of your parents. You even offered to helped out your siblings' children, too. Including your mother's sister and her children. That's greatness, Kai. Tell me who does that? The only question is, do they appreciate you? For 32 long years now, your mother is still under your care and living in your beautiful new home in Manila. You continue to provide well for your mother. You even helped her achieve optimum health and wellness, which none of your other siblings would care to do. Instead, they put all the responsibility on you since you are the one who excelled. It's not supposed to work that way with families, Kai!"

My only hope is that my family in Manila appreciates what I have done and understands it is not my sole obligation to provide.

I continue my cause and focus on another project, the Bridge of Hope Ministry, where I help impoverished children, remembering where I come from.

I want to be the voice for the oppressed. I don't like people being oppressed. I don't like people being put down. I don't find a reason why people must boast of their achievements and look down on others. When I see people being looked down upon or being mistreated, that's my biggest pet peeve. Unfortunately, there are some wealthy people who think and act as if they are immortal. Have you ever experienced being looked down upon? Have you been invisible to some high-up people who only mingle with their own race or status?

This is the main reason why I want to achieve greatness. When I do, I want to teach and educate people that the more we achieve greatness and good status, the more we must remain humble and grounded.

My motto is *give your very best*. Whether in life or business. Aim to be a great person or a great asset to the company you are working for. Become valuable to other people or your superiors. Serve them well. If they don't serve you back and treat you well, disassociate yourself from that kind of people or look for another place to work. Never sell yourself short. Whether in business or love, never sell yourself short. Make sure you get paid your worth. Make sure you are treated fairly. We have value and we need to make sure that when we give our best, it is reciprocated. If not, go look for someone who appreciates you as a friend or as a worker.

The only thing that matters is that you tried your best. Pursue greatness. Remember, it's the pursuit that makes a difference.

I remember my mother asking me, "Why do you help our relatives and other people who didn't treat us well? Don't you remember that when they were in a better status and we were down they were the ones who looked down at us, didnt talk to us and treated us as if we don't exist, never invited us to their parties and celebrations? We were invisible to them! None of them helped us."

And I replied, "But we are not like them."

Lessons from a Lion's Heart

- Don't measure yourself against others.
- You can be great in your own way. Embrace your own greatness.
- The path to greatness is traveled one step at a time.
- Achieving greatness does not mean you are above anybody else.
- Pursue to inspire, touch, and motivate individuals. Focus on serving others.

"With little to no resources, we can find ways to unleash our potential. Be happy with your own greatness — big or little as long as you impact people's lives. That is considered greatness."

Kai Hayes

Chapter 5

To Have and to Hold
We Need People Around Us

*"Surround yourself with only people who are going
to lift you higher."*

Oprah Winfrey

There are four men in my life who I hold dear in my heart.

Jesus, My God

My father, Cristino

My son, Nico

My husband, Greg

The most important things in life are the people.

God places people and opportunities right in front of you. It is important to keep your door open to any possibilities – like the possibility that the person who can potentially change your life as

God planned might just be knocking on your door. But if your door remains shut, you can miss out on something big.

Jesus and these three men all changed my life forever. They are now my "why's." Lion at heart is within me because they all led me to where I am right now, and my heart is on fire. I want to be the advocate to the invisible people who live such remarkable lives unknown to the world. It is time to be invisible no more.

*   *   *

Jesus is my ALL. My everything. Jesus rescued me from pitfalls. Since my innocence, I was already fascinated by Him. All I know is that I was born a Catholic. However, I choose to be spiritual than being religious. I love deep and profound faith rather than follow doctrines created by men. I observe a lot and meditate a lot, even at an early age. I observed people around us. I asked questions: "Why are we poor and others are wealthy?" However, those thoughts come in and out of my mind because all I know is that I am blessed to have a loving family that supersedes any inadequacy we have. Jesus got my attention. My faith becomes stronger as the years go by. Since then, I partnered with Him in all my future endeavors.

I am in the grip of Jesus; we all are. He is my "to have and to hold." He is my Refuge. My Rock. My Guide. He is the Lamp unto my feet. I could not picture my life without Jesus. We are all Jesus' favorites. The question is, is He our favorite? Whatever your faith is, our life is one great miracle. We all have special ways and understanding on how we recognize miracles in our lives. A miracle remains a mystery to the person who experiences one. You will recognize it when you have faith. For those who don't, they would think that success or good tidings are brought upon by themselves alone or because of their own merit.⁻

*   *   *

Cristino, my father, was my initial pillar in my early life here on earth. He was the first man in my life and has been the greatest influence on me. I am my father – mind, body and spirit. He taught me how to be generous, compassionate, and loving.

I am so like my father right now. Kai is the female version of Cristino. What I learned and absorbed from my father is his protection and love for his family, his assertiveness, being fun-loving, and humble in spirit.

He would say yes to life, opportunities and challenges, and figure it out later. That's what I learned from him. Say yes to opportunity and go figure it out to make things happen.

My father got his first job at 17 when he joined the Philippine Air Force. They needed a radio telecommunicator. He didn't know how to operate that equipment or what it took to hold that position. He didn't complete college. But guess what? He wanted to get that job, so he volunteered and then he figured out how to do it later. He asked people around him to train him. He passed the test and got the position.

Once, when he was in the military, a motorcycle escort was needed, an escort to the VIP group of politicians in the Philippines. My father didn't know how to ride a motorcycle. "Can you do this?" his commander asked. "Yes, I can." And my God, he learned how to ride a motorcycle on that same day and got the job as escort to the VIP. He's the most assertive person and the most street smart individual I have ever known. And that's Kai. I am going to figure it out.

My father was my protector, from the time I was born until I was a grown, young woman. I remember when I was around 18 years of age and began going out with friends. I always followed the rules in the house. My parents trusted me as I am not good at telling a lie. So, I would let my father know where I was going, who I was with, and what time I would get home. He would stay up until I returned, no matter how old I became.

I admired my father because he loved and respected my mother so much. His love for me and the entire family was unconditional. He would have given up his life for all of us. Aside from being protective, he was, on the other hand, the life of the party. He was a clown. He brought constant laughter and bliss to the family. However, as funny as he was, we all respected him. He knew how and when to draw the line. He could be like most famous comedians on the big screen yet, he could also be a knight in shining armor when he needed to be.

My father was someone to have and to hold. He was my rock. He was always there during my greatest struggles in life. Even in his afterlife, he mourns when I mourn. He laughs when I laugh. Now, that's a real ally! I trusted him 100 percent.

I had migrated to the U.S. just a year before my father died in 2004. We settled in Ohio for five years then later moved to Texas. I had brought my father and my mother once to the U.S. to visit me and Nico and see the new life that we had embraced in a new country and to see my new married life with Greg.

When my father died, my biggest supporter was gone. My inspiration. My protector. My hero. However, God called him home. If my father was alive, he would be so proud of me. And I know he is.

*   *   *

I got pregnant with my son in spring of 1992. I was thrilled! I am having a baby boy. I am going to be a mother. I didn't know what to do, honestly. I always feel numb when I am shocked and don't know what to do. Good or bad news, I will feel numb.

During my first marriage I was the main breadwinner. My ex-husband, unfortunately, was not a good provider.

My son was my biggest excitement as you can imagine. When I was pregnant, I only had four maternity dresses that I was alternately wearing to work. Even as I was nine months pregnant, I was still working and selling brand new cars for my clients. I had to save funds for my son. I was in bliss.

I now had my biggest "why." My son was growing inside my womb. The clock was ticking. I wanted to provide everything he would need when we welcomed him on earth. I told myself, he must have an air-conditioned room in our place, nice bedding, baby clothes, lots of toys, etc. I was still climbing the corporate ladder during those times. My future was still unknown. But there was no fear in my head. All I felt was excitement.

Nico came into the world in January of 1993. I was the happiest mother in the world. But I was in shock as much as I was in bliss. "I am a mother," I thought to myself. But being a mom for the first time, I was afraid to touch him. He looked so fragile, I thought I would break that tiny little body if didn't hold him right. My mother would teach me how to hold him and feed him with my milk. My mother was such a great help for my son. She is an expert. I thank God for my mother during those times because, honestly, I didn't know what to do. That precious little prince of mine is my biggest inspiration. The one who gave meaning to my life. To push forward. To achieve success. To win in life. When you have someone to have and to hold, the fear is invisible.

However, I was derailed from my mission when my marriage broke up. I was blindsided. I thought marriage was forever. I never thought I would marry a dishonest man. I asked myself, "Why do people lie? Why can't they be honest and break up first with the other person before carrying on an affair? Why wait until they are caught? Why hurt other people?" My first marriage really affected me negatively. I developed anxiety. I was human. Marriage is sacred to me.

I lost my self-esteem. I was broken hearted for years. The hurt and the pain I experienced was about my son. He was only three years old. What will I say to him when he grows up? I panicked. I was lost. I couldn't pray. Again, I was numb. No words or prayers came to my mind. How could this happen to me?

All I did for the most part was cry and cry and cry. Morning and afternoon. I couldn't eat, I lost 20 pounds.

A person can only cry so many tears, and eventually the lion in me was unleashed. Like my father, protection came to my mind. Not much time to grieve. My ex-husband hurt our son. I will not let anyone else hurt my son. No one will. I will do what it takes to prevent that.

I became a stage mother. I got overly protective because of what happened. "I will not trust any man that comes in my life," I told myself. I would not date. I focused on how to accelerate my status of living.

"No one will touch nor hurt my son," I often whispered to myself. For many years, that was my thinking, but that thinking was wrong. I became overprotective of him when he was little, and it didn't help that my father did the same to him. My father and I are alike. We are both lions at heart. We protect our tribe. I then realized only God can protect my son.

By the Grace of God, I've given my son the good life.

Those with the heart of a lion, we are warriors, we are fighters and that causes us to be very protective of not just ourselves, but the ones we love as well.

My son grew up a good child any parents would be proud of. He enjoyed his Confraternity of Christian Doctrine (CCD) Sunday class, his band, his soccer games, his singing in the choir, his new life in the U.S. My husband and I were able to afford to put him in private schools.

He has graduated with honors since kindergarten up to high school and graduated Suma Cum Laude from college. "The young man has a brilliant mind," Greg and I said to each other. Very analytical and cautious. The one thing I admire the most about him is his humility. He's very grounded. He is an introvert. He is funny. I love his dry humor. When he was little, I used to call him my *Dennis the Menace*. He loves pranking me. I trust and respect him. He trusts and respects me. Like his grandfather, he is very protective of me. We are transparent to each other. We have fun memories together both in the Philippines and here in the U.S.

He chose not to drink, not to smoke, not to try drugs. It was his choice. He is focused on education rather than partying. He studied interactive games design. That's the love of his life. He is developing and designing card games part-time with his peers. He loves traveling with his friends. He continues to travel locally and to other countries as part of our global business. Nico is the next victor.

When I started to put together this book, I talked to my son. I let him know that I was going to be telling people about my life, our life, our history. I asked him what this life I've led, being busy and traveling so much, has been like for him, and he wrote me this letter.

"I've always looked to my mother for as long as I can remember. She's told me stories of her hardships before and after my birth when I was young. I don't really remember any of the stories that involved me since, by the time I was past the childhood amnesia, I was mostly already living in a universe where I lived a comfortable life with my mom and my grandparents. At the very least, my mom was already on the rise in her success during our time in the Philippines. She was already the breadwinner at that point, but I did see parts of this journey moving forward.

My mom was already my hero, but growing up, that image of my mother only improved and solidified. How can I not look up to an incredibly successful businesswoman, beloved by her peers? Well, sometimes it meant she wasn't always at home and I remember loathing those times. I looked forward to the weekends because it was when there was the highest chance I could spend the most time with her after the long busy weeks she often had. The worst possible outcome was whenever she would go abroad. I always hated those times. Although, it did make me see my mom as this sophisticated, well-spoken, international traveler on top of everything else.

What really impresses me is how despite her busy schedule, I still feel she was highly present in my childhood. For each moment she wasn't there because she was busy working hard to support the family, a hundred more moments of fun spending time with her I would get back. She's always been generous with her limited amount of time. It extended past her immediate family too, which meant a lot of fun times for me with the rest of the extended family, especially my cousins. She's the person in my life that could do everything and anything even if life didn't seem to allow it; she could make the impossible happen. My mom was definitely the person I wanted to be like when I grew up.

Our new start when we first moved to Ohio actually allowed me to see the parts I didn't remember as a kid during her success journey. It made me appreciate how her success came to be in the Philippines, because at this point, she was on her way into another adventure to success. I saw more on what type of sacrifices she had to make to make things happen. The amount of determination and tenacity she would conjure almost from nothing was terrifying and incredible at the same time. Her ability to come back up from downtimes and hardships is what really put everything in perspective. All those times she seemed like an invincible woman to me when we were still in the Philippines, she wasn't. Yet, she still did actually do all of those impressive things. At any time, she could've just given up or quit. It wasn't guaranteed that she would succeed. Heroes always win and have a good ending, right?

While I enjoyed the times when she seemed like an unbeatable superhero when I was a kid, I appreciate it even more to know now that she was vulnerable the entire time, but still conquered failure like how an unbeatable superhero would. She did it all for her family. Yeah, my mom was and always will be the person I'd like to be when I grow up. But this time, I want to do it all for her. All the things she's provided for others, I want the same for her, you know? Personally, I think she deserves a lot more. I want to do my part, and what better way to emulate my hero."

— Nico

His remarkable letter moved me to tears. I brought up a beautiful person. He deserves the love I have for him.

My strong devotion to my son is why I was very careful in the choice of another husband.

*   *   *

My husband, Greg, is one of my four heroes in life. He met my expectations. If he weren't God fearing, I don't think that I would have a relationship with him. He was the person who I believe was the answer to my prayers. When I was in the Philippines, every day I would pass by the church and light a candle to Saint Joseph. I would say in my thoughts, "Dear Saint Joseph, no pressure, but I'm just lighting up a candle for you. If ever I would marry again, I need to find a righteous man like you. He's got to be loving and love my son unconditionally like you did with Jesus, and he's got to be a good father. He's got to be a good and faithful husband."

After five years of lighting candles and praying after work hours, I found Greg.

I had flown to New York for business to visit my principal company, *Easylink Services Inc.*, that I represented in Asia as an exclusive reseller for the telecommunications business. He and I met at one of the conventions in the U.S. We exchanged business cards, and I went back to Asia. Email was the biggest thing at that time. No Skype. No Facetime. He began to send me emails regularly.

However, he was one of the numerous men pursuing me at the time. Some via email, some men lived in Asia and pursued me in person. I was pursued by good and successful men, but my top prerequisite? Is he a God-fearing man?

I like communicating via email. God prompted me that I would meet the love of my life through writing. Whether you consider that real or weird, I am just being honest with my feelings. I listen and I believe in Holy promptings.

After ten months of exchanging thoughts, I got to know Greg on a deeper level. We connected through our spirits. Writing is powerful. Letters and poetry are two powerful and meaningful means of expression. Writing is the voice of an individual. If done in a proper way, creative writers emerge; brilliant poems and quotes have the potential to shape our way of thinking. In our case, we built a spiritual relationship that later flourished into a beautiful union.

It was an eye opener for me. I didn't know how beautiful it is to connect two people across the miles, expressing genuine thoughts through writing. Our communications grew deeper and deeper until I stopped getting acquainted with or meeting other men. I was never attracted to anyone else after that.

My communications with him were pure and genuine. It was a Holy experience. I gathered all our emails and they filled four thick binders. It was special. It was magical. His core values were those I was dreaming of in a husband. He was my miracle, he was Godsent. I knew I was guided.

When we realized we were falling in love, he invited me to come visit his place in Ohio. I refused. Instead, I invited him to come to Manila to meet Nico and my family. He did. The first man I ever invited to my house to stay. He was a perfect gentleman.

He met my entire family. Nico liked him. That was extremely important to me. He was accepted and well liked by everyone in the family. He passed the litmus test. Our first date was at a Spanish restaurant.

It was an enchanting evening. I felt good again. I was in bloom again. It had been years since I felt this way. Yes, I was in love once again.

At the end of his three week visit, Greg proposed. He memorized Tagalog, the language spoken in the Philippines, and proposed to my parents. It was brilliant. I didn't know it was coming. I was numb. I was in shock. I asked myself, "Is this for real?"

Everyone in my family was excited. Nico and his cousins were thrilled. It was like Christmas came early. It was a celebration! The most meaningful thing for me was when I saw my parents happy. My siblings were happy for me, too.

I wrote a poem for him:

A LOVE SO TRUE ...

Alone ...
In the long Winding Road
Searching for the Sun
Waiting to see the Light ...

There found a Love so True ...
Loving Spiritually and emotionally
An unconditional Love
Makes Joy Overflow...

Two Souls destined for each other ...
Across the Highest Mountains
Across the Deepest ocean
With Heavens Intervention
No one can Cease
A Love so true...

We were engaged for two years in a long-distance relationship. We managed perfectly. We alternately flew back and forth to see each other. Twice for me. Twice for him each year.

Our love story could be in the movies. I met his two beautiful children, Grant and Michelle. I love them. They are good children. They lived and grew up with their mother. I even met his ex-wife. She is a good mother to her children. She raised her children well. We are on good terms. Grant is the eldest, and Michelle is the youngest. Very humble kids. I love children, so it was easy to get along well with them. They are another blessing in my life.

Two years passed and I was faced with the decision of moving to the U.S. and marrying Greg. The plan was he would take Nico and me to the U.S. and start a new life. I would be a stay-at-home mom to spend time with Nico, who was 10 at the time. A decision had to be made. It was one of the most difficult and major decisions in my life.

I had not planned to live in the U.S. I was happy and fulfilled with my accomplishments and my career in the Philippines. I was running my own international telecommunications business. What more could I ask for? But when God has a plan for our lives, we can't insist on our own way. It was family and career in the Philippines versus a new relationship in the U.S. I prayed, "Lord, which one should I choose? I'm in a dilemma right now."

My discernment was crucial. But one thing was for sure, the prosperity that I achieved were all favors from God. God is LOVE. As a human being, I kept on thinking other thoughts. "What if this marriage won't work? If I sell my company, I stop earning. I will become a dependent, which I've never been before.

I would lose everything I've worked hard for." But one thing I know, where there is LOVE there is wealth and success. I chose LOVE. It was the best choice.

I took a leap of faith. I was afraid of the unknown. Prayers allowed me to find courage. That's why I took the risk of remarrying and migrating to the U.S. because I knew that I was doing the right thing. Greg is the man that I can depend on and trust. He is a successful corporate executive and a good provider. He is the replica of my father. He is as thoughtful as my father. He became my knight in shining armor. He is fearless like my father. He makes me feel safe like my father. My prayers to St. Joseph were heard. A funny aspect about my prayers is that Greg was baptized and confirmed at St. Joseph Church in Pennsylvania.

Greg became my father, my husband, my best friend, my confidante, my supporter, the biggest love of my life. The man of my dreams.

Our life is based on trust and that's the beauty of it. It took us a long time to develop that complete trust but when we did, it was solid. I have traveled alone for years, building our global business and we are at peace. We never doubt each other. We never give each other any reason to. We communicate constantly when I'm away. We call randomly and we see each other via camera. We are made for each other. Do we fight? Oh yes, we do. I think it's odd for a married couple not to argue. Besides, he is Irish ha! It would not be healthy if couples didn't argue.

He and I are both transparent to each other. I have found a person who I can trust my life with and my son's life, too. Even if I disappear here on earth, I know that my husband will look after my son. We are physically, mentally, spiritually yoked together.

We have been blessed for 17 years of marriage and it gets stronger each year.

*   *   *

Anyone can pray. Prayer is a time to speak your worries, questions, and concerns, and patiently listen in faith for the answers. Do the answers come right away? No. Will you hear a voice? Maybe, deep down in your heart; and it will be a knowing, a sure conviction.

To have and to hold pertains to many areas in our lives. A friend, a family member, a spouse, your children, business partners, or mentors can all be strong supporters. You must learn how to identify the right people to associate with.

When I began my career, I knew I had to start from the bottom. I developed the habit of observing how good leaders communicate, move, and act. I asked a lot of questions of them. I would listen attentively and heed their sound advice. As I sought better opportunities, their guidance helped me pursue the right direction or make good choices in life.

It's like I've got one slice of bread and a few chips on my plate. But what will I do with this? No matter what you have on your plate, you can create a more abundant life if you truly want to. All you have to do is connect with people who can mentor you for the better - those who instill good values and wisdom. We all need it.

Through prayers and meditation, and discernment, you can actually observe which people will help you. I have maximized these resources in order for me to reach where I am right now. You can, too.

Inspiration and mentorship can come from many other sources. Find books, speakers, and teachers who inspire you.

Listen to podcasts, watch interviews, and follow good leaders. Learn their skills.

It's like Robert Kiyosaki, author of *Rich Dad Poor Dad*, says, "Always remember that it's not money that will make you rich, it's business skills."

This chapter, To Have and To Hold, is about the significant people who inspired and mentored me in life – the ones who have helped me. Who inspires you? Who can mentor you? Who can you turn to?

Lessons from a Lion's Heart

- Good people can be the answer to your prayers.
- Spiritual faith can become your pillar to success.
- Seek out those who are willing to share their knowledge.
- Stay motivated by reading and listening to established leaders.

"When you pray, you will be guided to see the right people, say the right things, give the right kind of service, and make yourself valuable to others."

Kai Hayes

Chapter 6

Correcting the Errors of the Past
Nobody's Perfect, Make a Change

"Don't make your meditation about that person, thing or event in the past that holds you prisoner. Make it about your future self who is free of their past."

Dr. Joe Dispenza

'm always attentive. I'm always aware. Awareness is very important. We all must focus on self-awareness and be open to improvement.

It is human nature that we can't make all the right choices, so when we do fail or make mistakes, we better learn from them. Be observant. Be analytical with your life. As we push forward in our life, we must practice caution. If the people around you do not add value to your life, if they drag you to the pit, if they make your life miserable, then by all means do not be afraid to detach yourself from that relationship. Learn to draw a line and cut off any association with them.

We must continue to gain wisdom and understanding. We cannot continue to live a mediocre life. Personal, spiritual, and leadership growth is essential in life. When you keep going back in circles that means something is wrong with your choices.

Allow yourself to be mentored. Be open to constructive criticism from the person you trust. Continue to seek good and sound advice from your mentors and make sure you heed their wisdom.

Even though my mentors are criticizing or giving me opinions, they're still uplifting me. I welcome constructive criticism. I want to hear what they have to say so I can identify what areas I can improve upon.

Accept that no one is perfect and be willing to change.

When it comes to correcting errors of the past, I try not to allow myself to continue to make the same errors over and over. Maybe one or two mistakes are more than enough to help you grow and change, but if you're not learning from your mistakes and you're not willing to change and improve, then I believe you're not coachable.

You are not going to become a better person if you stick to your own thoughts and hold the opinion that you are always right. Self-righteousness has to be set aside, because if you really want to grow and you really want to improve upon your flaws and weaknesses and make an impact in other people's lives, you must be willing to make a change. If you want to be a good leader, a good coach, a servant leader, you have to first work on yourself and aspire to grow. Growing is basically focusing on what can you do to change those errors that you have made in the past to help you become a better person. When you are a better person you can lead others to do the same.

For example, my first marriage was unacceptable. But do I just blame my ex-husband for being a womanizer? No, I don't blame it all on him. Why did that happen? What did I do? Maybe we didn't have the same mindset? Maybe my personality was too strong for him.

He said to me once, "I'm only known as the husband of Kai Earnhardt. I do not want to be just the shadow of Kai Earnhardt." That's when I realized that he felt insecure because he was invisible. If he truly didn't want to be just the shadow of Kai Earnhardt, then by all means, he could have pursued his own greatness to help the family prosper. He didn't realize I was seeking success and growth for our own good. I was running a fast pace while he was taking it easy. We definitely were not looking towards the same direction. We were not a good match because we have different priorities in life. He took marriage for granted while for me it is sacred. I even recommended counseling, but he refused. Obviously, he was not ready to have a family.

I realized I needed to find a man who is confident enough to accept Kai for who she is. I run a fast pace and I am always leading my journey to success. I wanted to be successful. I didn't want to live a mediocre life. I wanted to create a lifestyle, to see the world, and I wanted to give to and bless my family. I reset my standards.

When I met my current husband, I saw the confidence in him I needed to support and help me to achieve a successful marriage. He supports me. He heals me. He's happy for my success. He does not compete with me. He gives me what I need to achieve my goals. He trusts me enough to understand my need to travel. He's very confident. We trust each other. We know that we're never going to be unfaithful to each other. That's the kind of relationship I wanted, and I tried very hard to be cautious and pay attention to the stop signs. He didn't give me any reason to not trust him. He didn't give me stop signs. I married the right man.

When making a decision, pause and think twice. Avoid being impulsive, especially in terms of marriage. It's a lifelong commitment, and sometimes, children are involved. Practice mindfulness. Always remember that mistakes are opportunities to learn. If you can afford it, work with a therapist to help you heal.

People make mistakes. It is human nature. First mistake, second time, third time, even a fourth time. However, if you can change for the better on the second time that would be great. If not, try harder because things have to change. If you continue to do the same things over and over, you are not learning from your mistakes. Whether in marriage or in other aspects of your life, work on correcting the errors of the past and avoid the same pitfalls in the future. We have the ability to change our path, to restructure our path and take back control of our life.

Purification. Cleansing. Starting all over again and making things new. Nobody is perfect, but I know in my heart that I am a better communicator now than a decade ago. Why? I've always wanted to change and improve my ways, especially in the way I handle conversations. Words can be powerful. I want to refrain from hurting people's feelings. Like others, I sometimes tend to be tactless. If I want to be a good leader, then I need to become aware of how I deliver and handle effective conversations. It was tough as I was climbing up the corporate ladder. I had to learn how to communicate positively with my staff and subordinates. If I wanted to inspire and uplift people, if I wanted to become an influencer, I needed to be cautious of how I use proper words. Words that speak of life. It is a special skill that people must continue to work upon.

In my previous careers I made numerous mistakes and bad decisions. There was a time when I employed a number of friends in my company with the purpose of helping them. I had to let go of a few of them for underperformance. They took it personally and our friendship suffered.

I learned to be cautious in hiring friends, no matter how much I want to help them. It's tempting to hire a friend or a family member when you have an opening in your business. You'd be helping them out and would get to work with someone you already know well, so it's win-win, right? Well, not usually. Here are three not-so-great things that often happen when you employ friends or family:

- Some expect extra freedom.
- Some give unwanted input and advice, which is hard to ignore and shut off.
- Some may not look at commitments as real.

As much as I wanted to keep my friends, some of them were not performing as expected. Some of them expected to keep getting paid. It was my first time running an Asian telecommunications business and I didn't know better. I learned this lesson the hard way and I became smarter and practical. Don't get me wrong; I'm not saying never to consider friends and family to work with you. Sometimes, we need trusted individuals to look after our business and in some cases, family is best. So, take this comment on a positive note. Since then, my business flourished when I hired the qualified candidates. I began making sound decisions and good choices. I shifted my thinking and developed a great mindset. Experience is by far the best teacher.

At first, I wasn't inspiring in my career. I read Dale Carnegie's book, *How to Win Friends and Influence People*, and it is now one of my favorites. Applying what I've learned, I developed the gift of inspiring people. You see, we all can change, we can be a better person especially if we strive for excellence. We may not achieve excellence right away, but it's the pursuit that makes a difference.

I'm now practicing to speak in a way that inspires people – to bring out the best in them. Validation and edification are such valuable assets. If we learn how to master these two words, we can help empower many lives. However, don't constantly dwell on your mistakes. Let your past life be a past life.

Some people carelessly commit the same mistakes over and over, while many others can't achieve excellence because they opted to be stagnant. They are petrified that they are going to make the same mistakes over and over. They are paralyzed.

My strong belief is that we all need to change. Take time to examine yourself and be open to yourself. We all need to learn how to identity where the mistake is coming from. Identify the causes and what needs to change. Gather information from personal experiences. Deeply examine yourself. If you're doing something wrong, evaluate what you did wrong and change things. Study and take notes from people who do well. Each of us should be in a constant search for people we admire and respect and whose behavior we can model.

Additionally, I've come to realize that one of the main reasons why people talk poorly about their past is because their present life isn't working. They feel safer talking about their past because they are afraid to step out of their comfort zone. Living in the past also validates all of the traumas, betrayals, and other negative experiences we've had in our life, and it is for most people such a great excuse for why they have not been able to change.

Unfortunately, if and when we make excuses for ourselves about something or someone, we are now giving away our power to that person, thing, or event in the past. As a result, we give away our power and ability to change.

"Each time you wake up in the morning and start to think about your problems, you are basically thinking about the memory of that problem. Our memories have emotion associated with them; the moment we feel that emotion, the body is now in the past."

– Dr. Dispenza

I just had a conversation with my son about his grandfather. As we shared our favorite memories of his grandfather, we began to cry, and the tears just overflowed. We miss him and all the laughter we shared with him. Our thoughts and language of our brain and feelings are the language of our body, so both of our brains and bodies were in the past. And after that we braced ourselves and put smiles on our faces and changed the topic of the conversation. Can you imagine if we continue to dwell in the past, talking constantly about his grandfather?

This is the reason why most people have not changed for the better. They remain sad. They cling to their past and blame the person or the event which caused their pain. When we keep our behavior like this, we become a victim and ultimately allow a person, thing or event to control how we think and feel. So, how do we break the cycle?

Allow me to share a few things that I've learned through practical experiences as well as through reading books to help me avoid living in the past.

- Keep records of negative thoughts and behavior patterns of things or events that you don't want to live by, so you can slowly leave the known and step into the unknown.

- Keep records of the new thoughts (the unknown) that you wish to wire into your brain. Begin thinking and visualizing about them constantly. Claim that you already have that in your thoughts and you'll eventually see the power of your thoughts. That is why it is important to think positively.

- Every day think of these positive thoughts and behaviors that you wish to develop. Establish these good habits.

- Meditate. Concentrate and keep your eyes closed as you do this. This prepares your brain for the future. It is not easy, but consistency is the key to achieving anything you want to change in your life.

- Each time you meditate, try to teach your mind emotionally what your future is going to feel like. Visualize it and don't stop practicing until you feel like that person you want to become. If you keep doing this, your past will eventually fall away.

In order to achieve personal growth, we need to focus on how to improve upon the mistakes that we made in the past. With that attitude and openness not only can we potentially achieve personal growth, perhaps we can also achieve spiritual and leadership growth. Are you willing to grow personally, spiritually and become a leader? Growth in many aspects of your life is truly amazing.

I cannot believe what I do now, who I am now based on my humble beginnings, where I originally came from, and who I was. It is quite an achievement for me. Surely there was growth. My secret is my lion's heart. When I'm hurting inside for various reasons, because of the many episodes in my tough journey, I break into tears. I cry. For me it's a sense of purification.

If I fail myself or I fail others, I acknowledge my fault and pray for forgiveness. I not only pray for forgiveness, but I forgive myself, then I reach out to the person I wronged and ask for forgiveness. I have no problem with asking for forgiveness from the other person. When other people have wronged me, I easily forgive, especially if I know that it was a genuine gesture. If forgiveness does not happen both ways due to a disconnect, I have learned to let go and know in my heart that I have prayed about it.

I connect with my heart for the most part. Then, I meditate and pray. Maturity is embraced when you are willing to correct the errors of the past. Let us be open to examining ourselves, identifying what we can do to change ourselves. Change begins in the greatest challenges.

There are some weaknesses that we all need to strengthen and improve upon. Don't just focus on your strengths, but also focus on improving your weaknesses, because it is truly amazing when we improve upon those flaws. Pursue improving your weaknesses.

Lessons from a Lion's Heart

- Change is a sense of purification, like a diamond in the rough.
- Be open to improvement. Do the work every day and do it with passion.
- Use positive thoughts and behaviors to establish good and better habits.
- Focus on what you can change to be a better and stronger person.
- Mistakes are opportunities learn and to change things for the better.

"Revival has to begin with SOMEONE; let it begin with YOU!"

Kai Hayes

Chapter 7

Ambition is the Fuel to Success
Breaking Through Barriers in Life

*"The best ambition killer is trying to play
someone else's game."*

Dan Sullivan

Most of us have ambitions and they are not difficult to give thought to, but the question is: Are you going to match your ambition with sacrifice? Ambition is our fuel to success. To be successful, you've got to have ambition, and that ambition must be powerful enough for you to sustain all the barriers that you need to break through. That's why **ambition equals perseverance**.

A lot of people tell me, "You inspire because you just continue to dig, dig, dig, and dig." I keep digging even when there are obstacles in front of me. Even in my current global business, my goodness, there were a lot of obstacles in front of me when our company decided to focus on other markets. When the Philippines operation shut down and most of my peers got hurt and quit, I lost a massive amount of sales volume. It was painful. I locked myself in the bedroom for a week. My dream of potentially achieving the top rank was shattered. The Philippines was a promising market. But what took place was beyond my control. Patience. Patience was required of me, and that was not easy. I braced myself and I continued with my journey. That's why I accelerated to a higher rank, while others chose to quit.

You've got to have a lot of ambition because human nature makes us all lazy. Ambition is the fuel to success. That's why we need to follow a structure. We need to follow instructions. Systems. We need a good system so that we can follow the road to success. Of course, there will be a lot of roadblocks, a lot of distractions, obstacles. If you're not disciplined, if you're not ambitious, if you are not willing to strive to reach the peak of your talent and reach that success, you're going to get frustrated. Frustrations can lead us to quit, to discontinue our quest. I admit I get distracted and frustrated too, at times. It's human nature, we all get distracted and frustrated, so make sure you know what you want, stay focused, and committed.

Ambition matched with perseverance is vital in reaching success. Many people quit early on. They don't know that perseverance can provide access to the things that help them to achieve success. Most people turn their backs easily on things they are pursuing because they can't resist the temptation of how it is easier to give up. It is easier to not do anything than continuing to push themselves and strive harder to accomplish their mission. They did not persevere enough to take the next step.

I agree that sometimes the hardest thing to do is to take a step. It boils down to how bad do you want to thrive? How bad do you want to change? How bad do you want to create the lifestyle that others have? It's all about the magnitude of your ambition. Of course, people quit and give up because there is no burning desire. There is no urgency either. But if you are set with your goals, you are ready with your mind, body and spirit. Especially with your true heart's desires. Then no one can stop you. It is simply non-negotiable. The ambition is set. You are focused.

Then it's like a car race, you are pressing the accelerator to the maximum speed in order for you to finish the track and win the race. That is what happened in my life. I always finish the tasks and reach goals I have put in my mind. Each time I win I create another goal to get to the next level. Next, after next, after next.

I remember my good boss at the bank called me his silver bullet. I asked him what he meant by that and he said, "You work like a bullet. Once you work on a task you are unstoppable." I like that because silver means lustrous and precious. And bullet means fast!

I am as hungry for personal and leadership growth as I am for spiritual growth. My mindset is always focused on winning. I've stumbled many times. It was not easy to get to where I am right now, but my hardships were fuel to my success. Why? They shaped me well. They prepared me mentally, physically and spiritually.

I am a cry baby. I love crying as part of my purification. It allows me to regenerate my strength. It is good for my soul.

Going back to our goals and ambitions, I believe it's a matter of asking yourself, "Would I rather quit, or would I move on and stay on the path?" What happens if you quit? Nothing's going to happen, right? It's a fact, but if you give it more push, there might be something that can happen. Again, it boils down to that people are fearful. People are afraid to fail, because failing for them is losing.

Afraid to fail? None of us, by any means, wants to fail. According to successful people and researchers, failure is actually good for us. We learn more from failure than success. It turns out that if we learn how to bounce back from failure, we discover an invaluable skill that will help us succeed. Again, for me, it's a platform for growth. And growth must always be our quest.

Not trying is truly the real failure. As you try and fail constantly, you have no idea you are probably near your success. Practice makes perfect, right? Therefore, failures must be welcomed. We must allow ourselves to experience failures.

You are a process. How can you get better at anything if you don't practice? You have to be bad before you get better, better before you become best, and best before you become exceptional. There's a process in everything. There's a process in building a team. Everything is a process. You are a process.

But we're talking about how to proceed. Most people become successful because of their attributes and that quality of perseverance. Consistency is a key to success as well. So be consistent. It is easier said than done, I agree. Let's find out how to stay consistent.

Staying consistent is hard because we tend to focus on the outcome or results more than the process. Put another way, we're more drawn to the positive feelings of outcomes rather than the struggle of the journey. Most of us quit during the struggle before we can experience the rewards of staying the course.

In order to stay consistent, champion your own cause. Find a good enough reason to fight for something. It better be nonnegotiable that you can't afford to get out of track! Ask yourself, "What is your great cause? What do you truly want to achieve?

What are you fighting for?" Then, and only then, can you achieve greatness!

When you identify your cause, make sure you are committed to putting every ounce of effort that you need to achieve your goals. Always ask yourself, are you willing to miss out on something to get that trophy? Are you willing to give it up for others to take it? Are you willing to miss out on something that, in the next five to 10 years, the project you are currently working on will become mainstream? If your answer is you are okay with missing out on all the examples above, then there is not enough ambition or fuel to seek greatness.

As for me, I always make sure I've got a full tank to go to my desired destination.

When I was a sales and marketing manager, I handled corporate accounts, so I had the privilege of sitting down with vice presidents, presidents and CEOs during my client visits. I was there to ensure they received quality customer service in order to maintain their loyalty. They were the decision makers and it was my job to provide them with a quality service that they deserve, with the hope that we would establish long term business relationships.

There are many things I have championed in my life with little to no resources. I believe I chose to set a better sail each year. I want to accelerate my life each year. I want to consistently grow personally, spiritually and leadership-wise. I want advancement in my way of thinking. No matter how small the improvement is, as long as I am not the same as the year before, I am good with that. I have accomplished my quest. Growth is vital for me.

On personal growth, I would never have written a book this year if I had not personally grown. I am not a writer by nature. I just challenged myself to write a book mainly because I believe that a book is an opportunity to use our voice for the voiceless. To inspire others to discover their own greatness and find the courage to thrive, to fight for and to encourage others to believe that we all can decide to stop being invisible.

Spiritual growth is truly about the person you are inside, your interpersonal relationship with God. Remember, nobody knows what's inside our hearts except for Him. What we see in a person is superficial. We often judge people based on their looks, and sometimes we discover their true hearts by taking the time to know them on a deeper level. Conversation is one way to know a person. Listening to them. Asking about their circumstances instead of merely talking about ourselves for the most part. I too, need to improve more in this area. I always strive to become a better person, not in terms of leadership achievement but as a Christian. We are all imperfect, but we can work harder to always give our best.

I get overwhelmed by what I have achieved throughout the years of my life. I came from nothing. I was an underdog and my whole family was too. First, I was able to prove to myself and to society that I can lead my family and put them on a pedestal. Then, I proved to myself that I can create, establish, and run a successful international telecommunications company without previous experience. Then, I proved to myself that I can build a successful global business. Then, I proved to myself that I can teach the right principles and behaviors to help others do the same. Lastly, I proved to myself that I can speak in front of thousands of people, which again, I had never done before.

Breaking through barriers in life is a difficult process we go through because the results are glorious.

These successes are all because of my ambition. Ambition is truly the fuel to our success.

Lessons from a Lion's Heart

- Ambition equals perseverance.
- Not trying is the real failure.
- Consistency is the secret to success.
- When ambition fuels your desire to succeed, you are virtually unstoppable.
- Experiences in life, good or bad, are the best teacher.

"Don't just watch people live their dreams. Follow them and learn their best practices. Then begin creating your own dreams."

Kai Hayes

Chapter 8

Surviving Versus Thriving
Finding Courage to Thrive

"The starting point of all achievement is desire."

Napoleon Hill

Surviving means living a mediocre life. For example, if you are living a life of poverty, surviving is being able to provide food on the table and a roof over your head for your family.

I was surviving in my early years, but I wasn't content with just getting by. I began searching. I began digging into my spirituality. Why am I created here on earth? Meditation helped me recognize that surviving is good, but what about other people? Why do they have better lives than I do?

I was always fascinated by great lifestyles. I read about successful people in magazines and watched them on TV shows. Then I started to look for the reasons why they were successful, and why my family wasn't. I thought a lot about the big difference between my family's status and other people's status. What are their secrets to success? Can I have success too? Or at least improve our lifestyle gradually?

I often asked God, "Why do people have different status?" Then I discovered that successful people have a lot of discipline. Successful people are willing to sacrifice. Not all of them are necessarily the most intellectual people on earth, nor do they have the highest education. I saw that the bottom line is, with little to no resources, if we focus on the tools that are available, and use those tools properly, like a system, a structure, we can be successful.

Without the structure, without the system, without the blueprint you can't put up a nice, wonderful house. Some people don't have a goal. They don't have a roadmap. They don't reach success because they're not committed to follow the plan. What I learned is to stay focused, disciplined, and use resources.

Don't be afraid to humble yourself and reach out to people who know how to pave the road to success. Listen to them. Accept the fact that you don't know everything, that you need to acquire more knowledge, and knowledge is power.

Do you want to survive or to thrive? Make a choice.

If your choice is to thrive, are you consistent enough to get back on track and then push yourself with or without someone pushing you? Or are you the type of person who can't focus?

Here's an analogy: You are on board a tourist bus in Europe. You are bound to visit a particular place you wish to see on that very day, and it closes at a certain time. But along the way, the bus is traveling along Paris' Champs-Elysees, one of the world's most famous streets. You get distracted and you tell yourself, "Oh, it wouldn't hurt to check it out for a brief moment and grab another bus shortly." You are tempted to hop off the bus.

Are you going to hop off the bus? Would you take the chance to miss seeing the place you planned to see that day? Most tourists, when they get off the bus, they never return on time and catch up on to the next bus hoping to reach their original planned destination. More often than not, they end up missing out on their plans. I was one of them. Stick to your plans. That way you will arrive at a well-designed destination.

Focus on your priority. Take back control of your life. People are so engrossed with the media, they don't know that they spend hours every day watching the media, the negative news. Even if we don't like what we see, let the media do their jobs. We can't control what is on TV. Focus on what you can control. Focus on how to become productive in life. What is your purpose? What is your role? Let the waitress do her waitressing job. Let the anchor woman do her newscasting. Let the actors do their movies. What is your role? Identify what your heart desires. Start investing time and money to support what you want. I want to be an inspiration, a motivational speaker. I want to bring light to people, especially people who are needing such direction that they don't know that they too can thrive. I want to give hope when hope is not in their lives. I want to be the voice for the invisible.

It's a matter of choice. It's a matter of decision. Little people can do extraordinary things. You don't need to be the most intellectual person. You don't need to have a Ph.D. or master's degree. Although it's great if you have it. You will have better leverage when you are highly educated. I am calling to those less fortunate who think they cannot contribute well in the world. The bottom line is, we each have unique qualities that we can discover and unleash. And when you do, ask yourself, "Have you contributed in this world?" Because life is passing. Have you pursued something that could make an impact in the world? Whether you fail, whether you become successful, it's the pursuit that always makes a difference. When you fail, relaunch and get back up again. You can unleash what you have in your own power that you think you can contribute.

I cry a lot when I am alone with God. I have a war room. It is inside my spacious closet. I collect crosses, rosaries, and prayer frames and place them on the wall. This is my sanctuary. When I am down, I go to my war room. When I am feeling defeated and exhausted, I go to my war room. When I need to pray for special people and friends, I go to my war room. I wear myself out crying for help. When I'm in despair. I ask God to fight my battles when everything seems beyond my control. Most of all, I also cry and run in prayers when I am simply grateful for the favors I have received from Him. I always find peace and solitude each time I go to my war room. When I come out, I feel rejuvenated. I feel ready to roar.

I understand that God has entrusted me to my husband, and I need to be a better wife. To my family, I need to be a better mother. In the community, a better citizen. On my team, a better leader. It is a huge responsibility. I pray for wisdom to be that person.

As our life progresses, we also need to be mindful of how we spend, how we fund projects, how we invest. It is not our wealth; it's God's. When we have an opportunity to travel in various places both local and international, whether business or personal trips, I contemplate and immediately send gratitude to God. In addition, I give all my effort and energy where it's needed. I never take God's gifts for granted. Remember, I didn't have anything in my earlier life, so I value every little gift.

Another thing I need to improve upon myself is my wellbeing. Sometimes I invest more in helping other people, and then

I forget to focus on myself. I hear about a problem; I try to fix it. I am a fixer. I've been trained to do that since I became the breadwinner, when I was a single mom. Sometimes I also have the tendency to overload my responsibility and exhaust myself. I forget to give myself a break to relax because I am in constantly focusing on thriving. However, I have learned when to take time off and when to rush. See? I am not perfect after all. Far from it.

This world is wounded. Many are suffering financially. In fact, how many of you reading this book are retired? Did you work 40–50 years? For some, perhaps more than that.

Where do you normally find the retirees? Cruising in the Bahamas? Unfortunately, no. Some we can find greeting people at Walmart. Some mopping the floor at McDonald's. The world has changed. Therefore, we need to shift our mindset now. Decide where you want to be – to survive or to thrive?

People who thrive in this world are the ones who are willing to adapt themselves to the new system, new idea, new technology, new platform. In other words, we all need to be open in learning and discovering new avenues for success. We need to push ourselves to take charge and lead or someone else will. Ask yourself, "Are you adaptable or closed minded?"

Are you willing and able to set aside the things that are not important, the things that will not benefit your life, your business, and your prosperity? Are you willing to set aside all the unnecessary things that will not be of value in your life, in your work, in your family, in your future? But, are you able to identify which one is significant and insignificant your life?

When you do, set those insignificant things aside. If you really wish to seek prosperity, you can achieve it. Everybody can achieve it. But it's just a little percentage of people who will definitely follow through.

You can read a lot of great books on wealth, on leadership and success, how to become a millionaire. Are you willing to put these great instructions and wisdom from these successful gurus into action?

I met a 40-year-old gentleman who works at the Apple store. He had an outstanding personality and provided excellent customer service. He got my attention with a little bit of talk. We had a sound conversation. He talks my language. I said he must be a visionary like me. I found out he has read almost 300 books on leadership. He has kept them all.

I invited him for a coffee to brainstorm and I discovered more about him. I shared my success story with him and really got his attention. He allowed me to mentor him. I took him to a few of my speaking engagements and leadership trainings. He spoke well during collaborations. Great mindset. He is brilliant. After all his questions were answered, it was time to make the choice. The decision. He said yes to joining my team. He is thrilled. He's got this. He wants to have what I have. Ready to sail.

I asked him the date and time he is ready to kick off. He began talking, "I need to renew my license. I need to fix my car. I need to go back to California to see my Dad for his birthday. Give me a week."

I spoke to him when he came back. He said, "I need to wait for the next paycheck. I need to clean this place for the meetings. I need to blah, blah and blah."

Simple. This is the reason why he is still working at Apple as a tech and salesperson after 15 years, doing the same things over and over. He is content in surviving instead of thriving.

Many people are intellectual enough to read good books, but they are still stuck in a rut, still in a hamster wheel, because they are not putting their knowledge into action. Is there some fear or is it just plain excuses? They don't know how to take the first step. Maybe they are overthinking and can't focus. Start by following through on just one step toward your future.

Most people are great starters, but they cannot finish the run. Why? No one wants to sacrifice. No one wants to feel the pain. One setback and they quit. Some of my peers quit. Quitting is the easiest to do.

Jesus didn't quit. He was crucified. He was distraught, but He prayed, in Luke 22:42–44, "Father, if you are willing, take this cup from me; yet not my will, but yours be done. An angel from heaven appeared to him and strengthened him. And being in anguish, He prayed more earnestly, and His sweat was like drops of blood falling to the ground." However, He went through with His mission to save the world.

Affliction visited our family. Stage 3 cancer struck. Greg, my husband, was facing agony. There was no cure for Anaplastic Astrocytoma.

I put a halt to my global business for six full months. I was by my husband's side each day. He needed me. We needed time alone. If I had lived a life of merely surviving, we would not have had the financial cushion that allowed me to stay home with my husband. By the Grace of God, he survived it.

I realized my mission is non-negotiable. I'm championing a great cause. I needed to enable my husband to retire and be home. I went back to work full force. No excuses were made. It was lonely traveling by myself alone. My only consolation during my trips were my global team. We enjoyed one another. I visited them to educate and train them. We attended conventions together. In four years, I achieved the leadership status in my global business, which allowed me to create a leveraged income. Then another four years, I accelerated in rank. Then, after one more year, my husband was able to retire. Success is a process. It takes time.

There are a lot of barriers in our lives. No one is spared. It will haunt you whether you're rich, you're famous, you're beautiful, you're ugly, you're old, you're young.

Don't let the barriers stop you. Break through, don't break down. Go back. Try again. When the door is closed, make sure you go around the back.

We will experience pain. We will experience distractions and disruptions. We will experience joy and bliss at the same time. But when the going gets tough, how will you face it? Will you quit? Will you fight?

What's making me strong? It's the faith and belief in myself. If others can do great things, I can do it, too. If one person can do it, another person can do it, and another person can do it, and another person can do it. You are that other person.

It only takes one person to create a movement. It only takes one person to prove that anybody can join and hop on board.

Ambition is the one aspect that will help make you thrive, because without ambition there's no path. There's no direction. Remember, ambition is the fuel to our success. There needs to be a great cause or inspiration behind that ambition. Why do you want this? Is it for you? Is it for your family? Is it for your spouse? What inspired you to have this big ambition? Dig deep into your heart and identify what you want to champion in life.

I was sick and tired of seeing my parents being stepped on and not included. Sick and tired of hearing that we don't have money to pay the rent, no money to buy things, no money to eat what we want to eat, or do what we want to do. If this is the measurement of how most people are invisible, always excluded, and don't have a voice, then let me try being successful. Let me try to see the other side of the fence. See what it looks like. See how it feels being there. I realized that being successful and having that wealth makes a big, huge, massive impact because humans are very materialistic. There are things I don't like that other successful people have. Arrogance. Hunger for power and attention. Cliques. Hypocrisy. I feel uncomfortable around those types of people.

You must set a good example so that you can be a beacon of light and bliss. You can be the example of putting others onto a pedestal and helping others to achieve what you have achieved. Serve. Inspire. Remember where you came from. Remember, your victories and accomplishments are God's favors. We can't attain our successful status without God's grace.

My husband and I were sent on all-expenses paid trips by our principal company in various beautiful places like Bahamas, Ireland, Hawaii, and many others to participate in leadership events. We were there to celebrate with other top achievers, and it was an extraordinary experience for both of us. That's what God has in store for those of us who work hard and put forth the right efforts. Rewards. Incentives. We are always grateful. I am and will always be especially mindful of where I came from.

Thriving is success for me. However, you need ambition and discipline, and you've got to have a certain system and structure, because even if you read the book, if you don't have the system, if you don't follow the structure, you will fail. You won't thrive.

Yes, I am a very competitive individual. I admit I was money-driven, because I not only wished to survive, I wanted to thrive in everything. Whenever I realized I wasn't getting paid for the outstanding quality service and performance I provided to a company, I would seek another company who would be willing to reward me with an acceptable wage and improve my status.

Anyone can thrive. Connect with your heart during quiet moments. Take time to meditate. It's where you get the strength back.

Lessons from a Lion's Heart

- Always choose to thrive. Learn to adapt yourself in every situation in front of you and discover new avenues for success.
- Don't be afraid to breakthrough barriers ahead of you.
- Shift your mindset, adapt to new things.
- Discover courage to unleash your unique qualities and talents.
- Self-discipline, focus and sacrifice lead to thriving.

"Ask yourself, do you want to continue to live and exist or flourish and live your dreams?"

Kai Hayes

Chapter 9

A Life Neutralized by Prayers
Attaining Equilibrium in Your Life

"Show me your prayer life, and I will show you your destiny."

Paul Brady

Why is it significant to live a life neutralized by prayer? It is to acknowledge God and deny arrogance.

Curious of who God really is, I began reading the Bible when I was in college. Through immersing myself in the Bible, I began to know Jesus. I welcomed Him in my life and acknowledged Him as my Savior. Life continues to happen. I grow deeper in my faith. I learned that no one is spared from obstacles, adversities, trials and hardships. However, with Jesus in our life, favors, grace, blessings, good tidings, and protection will flow to us as well.

What is a life neutralized by prayer? What do I mean by that? For me, **neutralize** means obtaining balance and equilibrium. No one can do great things on their own. We all need people around us – people who raise our standards, people who support our cause or simply serve to inspire us to move forward in our journey. More so, we all need God in our lives. If you do not have God in your life, find Him. I did. I ignored His call for many years until I learned to acknowledge His presence and put Him on top of my life. I later became much stronger fighting against all odds. As I get defeated, I just find myself standing stronger and moving on. He is my constant companion. He was there during my hours of frailty. I began acknowledging His presence and accepted Him as the lamp unto my feet.

There are benefits of living a life neutralized by Prayer:

- *Personal Transformation.* Fervent prayer changes us in a positive way. Some of the greatest miracles come at the greatest cost. Therefore, it is good to not allow laziness to get in the way of our prayer life.

- *Divine Revelation.* Not only do we get changed, we faithful believers witness the promises of the scripture come alive within us. The way to prosperity, healing, and breakthrough that are written on each page of the Bible become real in our lives with prayer.

- *Spiritual Rejuvenation.* We all get burned out. I get it, but the difference between the weak and the strong is the weak have the tendency to retreat from prayer, while the strong run to prayer. Make prayer a routine, do not stop praying. Pray more.

- *Demonic Elimination.* When we pray, demons, curses, and negative thoughts such as lies and doubts get eliminated. One key result of a lifestyle of prayer is a victory over the enemy.

We need armor. We need to wrap ourselves in the full armor of God. We need the right ammunition. We need not only prayers, but the exact resources and tools to get through life. We should know how to use the tools and knowledge the right way, the proper way. Just as in battle, you need to be skilled. You need to have the full armor – physically, mentally, and spiritually - to fight and win. If not, you will become a casualty. Perseverance and tenacity are the key.

Are you going to be lazy or are you going to have belief in yourself? You need your faith. Stretch your spirituality. That is why a life neutralized by prayer can move mountains.

Prayer is my foundation, my constant. My faith has grown deeper as I grow older. And it feels good. It is refreshing. It does not mean I do perfect things all of a sudden. No. But as I accelerate in life as well as in business, I also desire and love accelerating in faith. I learned how to acknowledge God's favors in silence and offer thanksgiving. I take the time to be thankful for every success in my life, the small ones, the big ones. I take the time to thank God including the people He brought into my life. I ask Him for His outpouring of love, strength and courage during my darkest hours.

Every time I am faced with making challenging decisions, I turn to prayers. I consult through prayers. Prayers can come in many forms. If I do not have words to utter because I am numb and in shock, it is as simple as, "Jesus, You know my heart is in agony, lead me the way for I trust in You." Prayers give me discernment. Not to say I always make perfect decisions, but fervent prayers result in wisdom and understanding.

Maybe some people call it meditation. That is as beautiful as prayer. I probably consider myself more of a mystic (generally associated with the belief of experiencing union with the ultimate Divinity, Spiritual Truth or God) than religious. I love talking to nature. I love being in the park. When the wind blows while I am praying, that means God is hugging me. When there's chirping of the birds where I go, I experience bliss. When I find myself in quiet places, I find solitude and peace. I love that because I want to connect with Mother Earth. God created our universe. Let us savor its goodness. We all must find solitude in our lives in spite of the fast pace we live in to attain equilibrium.

Prayer has also taught me how to be patient. I prayed for a Godly man to come into my life. I prayed for someone who would be right for me – someone who would also be right for my son. I prayed for years, lighting candles each afternoon after work when I passed by the church.

On the seventh year, I remarried. Looking back, my decision to marry Greg and emigrate to the U.S. was a huge one.

I prayed to God. He said LOVE is above all. God is LOVE. That is my choice. I was ready to leave the lifestyle I had spent years building – for one good reason, I found the love of my life. I took a leap of faith, and God blessed me.

Prayers allowed me to clearly see a difficult decision. I received discernment. Prayer showed me to choose love versus wealth (my successful business in the Philippines). Remarrying was a huge risk. I gave up my entire life in Asia where I grew up and lived for 40 years. I left my parents and family behind, taking my son to the U.S., away from his grandparents and cousins and friends, choosing to start a new life. I sold my Asian Telecommunications business where I achieved financial success. These were all the moving parts of a massive decision. Emigrating to another country with no friends, no job, no business. Facing the unknown. I could not have done any of this without the power of prayer.

A life neutralized by prayer is powerful.

In the journey that is our life, we will all experience pain. We will experience destructions and disruptions. We will experience joy and bliss as well. Life happens to all of us.

Pause for a moment and capture that voice within you.

Talk to yourself. Meditate. Pray. Talk to the highest form of yourself. Then, sit quietly and listen. When I do this, it allows me to get the answers to my questions. It's kind of like this mysterious guide, an inner voice speaks to me. We all have that voice. The key is to be quiet enough to listen, and then believe we will be guided in the right direction.

It is human nature to be impulsive, to do things that are driven by the desire of the flesh. Temptations follow our life everywhere. Thus, one needs to attain balance in life. We need to protect our flesh as well as our spirit. Because, if and when our flesh turns into darkness, our spirit suffers. To neutralize means to render harmless, to obtain balance or equilibrium. When I say I live a life neutralized by prayer, it is because I have come to recognize that prayer allows me to calm down, make me consider the consequences that might be harmful to me and my future. Certainly, I have no desire to continue making the same careless mistakes I did in the past. We all need to grow spiritually. Aspire to become a better human being. Prayer allows me to discern things, especially in making decisions. Impulsiveness is neutralized by the act of prayer. When we render a situation harmless, we have contributed something that can help the world to heal.

I still feel inadequate at times, even going on the stage. I feel inadequate because I tend to compare myself to others who deliver such exquisite performances. I acknowledge my limits. I am not as profound and polished as are many others. But guess what? When I stood up in front of the room with thousands of people, I felt victorious as my speech moved the audience to tears. That's when I concluded that prayer matters. I prayed that I would provide value and inspiration as I delivered my speech. I was more concerned for my audience than myself. I desired a compelling message that can be remembered for years, not just during the moment.

The whole glorious and unexpected experience melted my lion's heart. It changed me entirely and even allowed me to dig deep into prayers and meditations. From now on, all things in life must be focused towards growth in all aspects and serving others. Focus on the quest for lifting the spirits of human beings and help unveil the lion in their hearts, ultimately making the world a haven of peace.

Humbling words from my audience as I came down from stage was immeasurably moving to me. I don't take things for granted. I listen attentively.

"You moved us."

"You delivered a compelling message."

"You were an inspiration."

"You put us to tears."

"You were anointed."

"You changed my perspective on life."

Now, these overwhelming comments made me break down in tears. It was truly a humbling experience. I was not worthy. The most important thing people didn't realize was, receiving those powerful words, they have moved me, too. They have changed my life forever. My prayers were answered. I wanted to be a better person. Some people's prayers were also answered through my speech as they were inspired. A true work of God. For me, it was one great miracle.

Sometimes all it takes is one good book. One good book can touch people's lives. A book that takes you on a journey of various experiences good or bad. Suddenly, a window of opportunity is found in a book that can potentially change your life. I'm not saying it is this book, or that this is the only book, but suppose it could be? Suppose this book could potentially transform your life?

With every success, even every little success, learn to take time to be grateful. Expressing gratitude is a sign of humility and meekness. Whether you're rich or you're poor, we all go through things in life. There is no one, no single person who is spared from afflictions. The greatest equalizer is sickness and death, yet prayer makes a difference in our lives.

Lessons from a Lion's Heart

- Spirituality is a gift. Stretch your spirituality.
- One needs to attain balance in life through prayers.
- Acknowledge God and deny arrogance.
- A life neutralized by prayer can move mountains.
- Recognizing that higher power is a sign of humility.

"Why do I always find the courage to overcome obstacles in life? It's because Jesus is my partner."

Kai Hayes

Chapter 10

Sharing Your Gifts with Others

The more you give, the more you receive

"For it is in giving that we receive."

St. Francis of Assisi

Giving is one significant measure of greatness that is truly universal. It is a measure that goes beyond human race, age, sex, color of skin, culture and wealth. Greater love is giving and sharing your gifts with others. In any state of life, the crucial point is really one's ability to deny themselves and think of how they can be concerned with other peoples' difficult and challenging circumstances.

This book *Lion at Heart* led me primarily to honor the four men in my life. Jesus, my father, my son, and my husband. These four men not only inspired me to write this book and share my humble journey to success, but also gave me the courage to break through all the barriers in my life. They were my instrument to pursue great things by helping and serving people.

In addition, people in this world simply inspired me to write this book. You, who are reading this book. People who are invisible just as I was when I was growing up. My whole family was invisible in this world and I was determined to end it. I want to become an ambassador to help individuals to rise up and decide to be visible. Invisible people are the impoverished, the elderly, the chronically ill, orphans, and the wrongly accused. I acknowledge their existence and the great value and life lessons that they can contribute to all of us through their sad or remarkable stories. The invisible people can also discover the lion in their hearts and become warriors in life. As for me, I have sought financial freedom all my life to help my family live a good lifestyle and inspire others to do the same.

You can make an impact. You can touch people's lives. Be an inspiration to the uninspired. Give hope to those who feel hopeless. Enough of profoundness. Just be yourself. People identify where your heart is. Bottom line, it is about pouring your love into all. Love is above all. Love is God. I will focus on my heart. That is why I wrote this book. To share my utmost and deepest love with all my readers.

We can help heal the wounded hearts by sharing our triumphant stories.

Words are powerful. By reading, listening, then sharing our stories, we can reach out to thousands of wounded individuals who just need to hear a heartfelt story. A compelling story can touch many people's lives. If we can make a difference in a person's life by sharing our stories one at a time, we can help make this world a better place.

Be aware of your success but maintain humility. Some people zoom into success and they forget everything. I always try to be aware of my various experiences, my successes as well as my failures in life. I keep a record of them and use these records as a tool for my growth and helping others.

Creating a lifestyle from poverty is a huge transformation in my life, thus, I wish to express gratitude, give acknowledgement, and show appreciation to all the people who are a part of my success and my inspiration to reach personal, spiritual, and leadership growth. It was indeed a tough and long journey. But it allowed me to meet the right people as the inspirations for my success. These were people I could run to when I needed comfort as I continued my difficult journey in life. Year after year, I see myself immersing into a great new life, a better one, because I discovered courage and greatness within.

I am grateful for my drive to bring myself up out of the life of poverty. I was committed to my cause. I am grateful for the ability to take care of my parents and grandparents. I am grateful for the dignity I was able to give my family. I am grateful for the opportunity to live my life as an example to others, that I can inspire people to know that they too can rise. They can rise above poverty. They can rise above their situation no matter what it is. They can build and put legs on their dreams. If one can do it, another can follow. I've been there, and I am telling you there is a way out. *Right now*.

Now is a good time to sit quietly and reflect on the people who have guided your life. Here is your opportunity to express your gratitude. You can thank God for placing these people on your path, or you may choose to reach out to someone and express your appreciation.

Another way to express gratitude is to offer up help to someone else. We all have knowledge and skills that can benefit others. Who can use your help today?

To date, I still provide for my mother; the others have passed away. My mother is currently living in my new beautiful two-story home in Manila with Remy, my ever-trusted adopted family. She is another blessing in my life. To have and to hold.

As you remember, my siblings left all these obligations to me. So unfortunately, their limiting belief of not having the means to help support our parents and grandparents in the past 32 years led them to become stagnant in life. Like them, I didn't have the means to take responsibility and become the breadwinner for the family, but I took the challenge without hesitation. God provided and filled in the void. When there is a will, there is a way. I trust that my siblings realize that when we give, we receive. I just kindle such a hope that my help is valued by those people who received my support. I'm not sure. The one thing I know for sure is that we cannot please everyone. Some families, as you know, are tough. Sometimes your heart must be ready, as your unconditional gift can be often overlooked and suddenly becomes an obligation. However, we must continue to love them all. We must continue to help as we can in all circumstances. For a true gift must be unconditional.

But a lion at heart must have boundaries. Give what you can give. Help how you can help. It's up to others to value your help or not. By always giving to people financially, they lose the opportunity to take a stand for themselves. When you are wounded and pull yourself up, you can teach others to do the same.

Even a lion's heart gets wounded. Accept that not all people appreciate our good deeds. It can become painful, especially if no one realizes how we feel. I get it. It's human nature; people are selfish. We all have that selfish nature. We all have the tendency to be concerned about our own feelings. I am guilty of that as well. However, let love and forgiveness prevail.

In my opinion, do everything out of love. If that is not acceptable to the people you love or serve, leave it at that. There is nothing else you can do. Be at peace. That's what I did. I have learned to let go. Through the years, it took a toll on me. Some people I couldn't make happy no matter how much I tried. I'm good with that. My ability to help others was made possible because I chose to sacrifice and work hard. What I gave was a gift. What they do with that gift is up to them. If people appreciate me, great. If not, all good. We are all humans. Oftentimes, we do not know that we are hurting the feelings of others. I may be hurting someone right now by opening up my heart and revealing my thoughts and real feelings. I ask for forgiveness. I intend to hurt no one. The moment we express our inner feelings, we become vulnerable to being judged because most people expect that when we learn and begin to preach goodness, we are no longer capable of making mistakes. That is not true at all. We are not perfect, we will never be.

Begin right now giving your time to others. No matter what the circumstances it brings you. Giving is an act of love. Giving is serving others. Do not expect anything in return. Give tools and resources to people. Share your life's journey or story with those who need to hear it. Share your knowledge. Identify the right people who want to make things happen. One of the beautiful things I embraced in my current industry is that entrepreneurship teaches people a skillset they need to improve their life. Once learned, no one can take that knowledge away from them.

Being a lion at heart is being able to pull yourself up by the bootstraps, taking your circumstances and turning them into gold and opportunity. It's a different mindset. It's a total paradigm shift. Support your family or friends in building the skill sets to achieve their own abundance. What matters is someone's willingness and ingenuity.

There will always be some people you can't please. But hush and know that even Jesus didn't please everyone. If you allow these negative people to disrupt you, then you're on the losing end. You only get hurt by people when you allow them to hurt you. For me, I just focus. For as long as I do not intend to harm or offend anyone, I am at peace. All I'm focusing on is to help and serve. I told myself I better be cautious on aspiring to become a good leader. I need to understand that to be a good leader, one must understand and be willing to serve, not to be served. However, it is important for a servant leader to continue and move on with powerful boundaries in place. We deserve respect.

Mother Teresa provides the greatest example of servant leadership, showing that we truly do not need the power of wealth and materialism. We just have to speak. We just have to have a voice.

No one had fewer resources than Mother Teresa. She started on her own with the direction and guidance of the Holy Spirit. She knew her purpose was to be the voice of the people who are wounded and who are lowly. Then the successful people became supportive of her. She attracted people. She didn't have social status, but see how fate kicked in? Fate can lead you.

"It is not how much we do,
but how much love we put in the doing.
It is not how much we give, but how much love we put in the giving."

Mother Teresa (*No Greater Love*)

Mother Teresa was born in 1910 in Skopje, the capital of the Republic of Macedonia. Little is known about her early life, but at a young age, she felt a calling to be a nun and serve the Lord by helping the poor.

She joined a group of nuns in Ireland and then was given permission to travel to India. She began working as a teacher which led her to start the *Missionary of Charity*. She experienced two particularly traumatic periods in Calcutta. First was the famine. Second was violence. For many years, Mother Teresa and a small band of nuns survived on minimal income and food, often having to beg for funds. Slowly her efforts with the poorest were noted and appreciated by the local community and Indian politicians.

"Not all of us can do great things. But we can do small things with great love."

Mother Teresa

Through her extraordinary religious work and ministries, she was awarded the Nobel Peace Prize in 1979 "for work undertaken in the struggle to overcome poverty and distress, which also constitutes a threat to peace." Mother Teresa became a saint, offering a great example and inspiration to the world.

May her story of sacrifice, determination, and generosity inspire you the way it has inspired me to unleash my lion's heart.

Lessons from a Lion's Heart

- Share your story with others so they may be inspired, and take courage to do great things.

- Share your bounty of resources and knowledge, that others may benefit and grow.

- Helping can be in the form of teaching rather than gifting.
- The ability to help others requires true sacrifice and hard work.

"There is no greater love than to express gratitude, give acknowledgement, forgiveness, and show appreciation to others."

Kai Hayes

Chapter 11

You are the Author of Your Life
Discovering your Own Greatness

"Every man is the architect of his own life. He builds it just the way he wants it. However, after he has built what he wants, he sometimes decides that he doesn't like what he has built and looks for someone or something to blame instead of changing himself."

Sydney Madwed

When we were born here on earth, I believe that we are born with a purpose. No one is born without a purpose. Not every one of us knows what our purpose is and that's why we have quests. It is not always easy to find our purpose at an early stage. We all need to go on an expedition. Exploration. Explore your life to the far horizon, hoping to find meaning. The meaning of life.

What is life? And how can anyone put meaning to it? Life can be short. Sometimes, it could be shorter for those whose life is significant and could be too long for those who see life as inconsequential. For me, life is what you put meaning to.

When I am in solitude, I ask what meaning my life really has. Sometimes, I feel like I know, but many times, I feel like I don't know where I am going. I just don't see the road ahead of me. Do you feel like that at all? Life is just massive, so full of unexpected moments like a mystery. Even before I can put meaning to my life, part of it is gone and the meaning I try to put is already drained.

As Father A. Arboleda puts it, "Life, it seems, is like dry sand slipping through your fingers. When you try to hold onto it tightly, it begins slipping away faster. But when you try to throw it away, it sticks to your hands." He said, "To appreciate life best, perhaps you should not try to either hold on to it tightly nor to let it go carelessly. The sand in the hourglass is life. It is better to let it flow freely." However, we also need to focus on things that last and could potentially have real meaning in our life.

Back then, I began my spiritual journey when I was 35. I was given a great favor to own and run my first company in the Philippines. I was a single mom who took a major responsibility, being summoned to be the breadwinner without proper planning or resources. Oftentimes, how we take life is dictated by what priorities we have. Life offers everything which can be our priorities. Like in my case, who was ever eager to get out of poverty, I would say, "Life will be meaningless if my family and I continue to move from one shack to another." Or a terribly in love man would say, "Should I lose her now, life would be meaningless to me and therefore I have no reason to live." Or a young ambitious businessman who desperately wants to make his first million before reaching 40, dies at 39 and never spent quality time with his wife, children and family.

As I grew older and acquired wisdom, I began to be careful with my decisions. Yes, I had the quest to become financially successful but at the same time I was solid with my faith and reputation. I set clear discipline to which direction I am willing to take when faced with making a choice. I cannot allow myself to always go and follow where it glitters. I examine my heart and make sure my heart feels good in terms of discernment. Many of us are faced with diverting roads. It can be tricky. One road can be a short cut to anything you desire in life but only offers temporary gratification. The other might take a longer route and require hard work, but it can be more gratifying in the end.

Remember, when I started my life journey, I was money-driven because I was responsible for the lives of my family. It was the scariest time of my life. But never, ever did it come to my mind to remarry for convenience. I could have made that choice, a short cut, as I was pursued by several admirers when I was a single mother. I was good looking. I was once a model, remember?

Indecent proposals were outpouring. Because my integrity and respect for Jesus is solid, I turned down those proposals even though some of the offers were attractive – a luxury apartment, a car, jewelry, funds for my parents and most especially for my son. Wow! That would have been the easy way. But no way! In the Philippines, many women are offered this kind of proposal, especially if they are good looking. Men are outnumbered. The ratio of men to women in the Philippines is 1:6. Meaning one male to six females. This type of proposal is most common in that country. But, being a kept woman was not an option for me. I know Jesus was delighted with my choice.

The main reason why I chose to create my own journey in life, choosing to create my own story and become the author of my own life, was brought upon by individuals who hurt me and my family in the past. I grateful to them for they unleashed the lion in me. In my own humble opinion, nobody has the right to misjudge and castigate others for not having valuable things in life. One must begin to value goodness. Become a good example by teaching others that no one can boast of one's achievement compared to God's standards.

Go for your quest. Fight for what you are fighting for. And when you reach success, do not take revenge. Instead treat people with kindness. It can help transform people for the better. I remember vividly the pain it brought in my heart when my parents and I were living in my brother-in-law's home. We were not allowed to come out from our room or make loud noises each time my brother-in-law's family came to visit. My sister opted not to be the voice for the voiceless. It was devastating.

I took all our past unpleasant experiences to heart and began to dream. And when the wheel turned upside down, and my brother-in-law lost everything, I was his refuge. He was so gracious to send gratitude each time he asked for financial and emotional support. We developed a good friendship in the end. I saw his good side because I opened my heart to him. Sadly, he passed away a few years ago, but I still keep his meaningful and gracious text messages to me. I often read them when I reflect on life.

Everything, every decision in our life boils down to our mindset and decision making. What do you want to settle for in life? Who do you want to become? We have been given the ability to turn our life around. We are in the driver's seat. We are holding the steering wheel. Which direction would you like to steer your life?

You are fearfully and wonderfully made and created by God. By the Grace of God, each of us has been given a certain talent, perhaps numerous talents. How are you going to discover your talents if you are not willing to go on an expedition? Life is all about discovery. It is a great expedition. No one will dictate where you want to go except you. Isn't that remarkable?

When we reach the age of 18, we are given the freedom to explore. Go out there. See the world. It's not like in school where everything we do is structured and dictated. Whether you achieve, college or not, life goes on. Move forward and don't look back. You only look back to remember where you came from. That is, to determine how much you have grown. Definitely, you will become are a different person now than who you were before. Value everything that you achieved. Little or big. That's who you are. Throw away your bad habits. Be willing to correct the errors of the past. Make all things new in your life as Jesus did in the world.

Always remember that life is full of risks. A good foundation in life plays a vital role for the most part. A good, solid foundation normally helps a person live a life of prosperity and abundance. But if not, find the missing link. Identify and strengthen your weaknesses. You can carry these core values with you as you walk through life. Go for gold. Aspire to win.

Always remember, we all experience seasons. There comes a time you will experience long winters. Darkness along the journey. That is why I instilled in the earlier chapters that meditation and prayers are essential in our life. It is a lamp unto our feet. Why? The world is wounded. We are all patching holes in our lives. As we are wounded or in pain, life offers many temptations. Life offers vast easy ways out. We live in a material world. We live in constant pressure.

Some homes and workplaces are no longer secure places. What counts are the values we discover and ultimately make our own. To discover which is the right model, we must look closely into our hearts. If we do, we can potentially discover passions that are either constructive or destructive. Our capacity to love or to hate, to give or possess, to build or destroy, to forgive or to avenge. But if we cling to what is positive and shun the negative, we will definitely discover what model or example to embrace. Ultimately, we will discover the meaning of life. Are you fully equipped to discern?

Thus, mental, physical, and spiritual maturity is needed. Maturity will guide you as you take the leap of faith. Do not be paranoid. Do not anticipate failure. Just enjoy the journey. Find and do things that make you happy, as long as that happiness does not destroy other people's lives. Observe moderation. Choose the people you want to associate with.

If you want to be the author of your own life, then apply all the chapters of this book to your personal journey.

One must be willing to **Walk Through Darkness** to get to the next morning. No pain, no gain. We are all diamonds in the rough until we polish our potential with hard work and sacrifice. When we overcome darkness in life, we become the child of light not the child of darkness. Then, let us shine like a beam of light.

Victories over Sacrifices. Know that victories can only be achieved through massive sacrifice. I have not known anyone who became victorious who was not willing to sacrifice. Victory does not come easy. Be willing to record events that happen in your life from start to finish, and only then, will you realize that victory equals sacrifice.

Mission and Vision. State your mission and identify your objectives. Have a clear vision and identify your why, what you want to accomplish. Create a road map to success. Focus on your quest. Execute the proper guidelines. Mark your freedom.

Pursuit of Greatness. Don't measure yourself against others. You can be great in your own way. Remember that doesn't mean you are above anybody else. Take one step at a time, be consistent, and never give up until you reach your goal. Pursue to inspire, motivate, and serve others. Whether you achieve your goals or not, it's the pursuit that make a difference. Then relaunch your goals.

To Have and to Hold. Look for a mentor. Reach out and don't be afraid to admit you don't know it all. Be grateful to those who support you physically, mentally and emotionally. It could be a friend, a partner in life, a business partner, your children, your family. Most of all, cling to God. Partnerships are your best weapon to protect you from the enemies of this world. We all need people around us. People who help us to become a better version of ourselves.

Correcting the Errors of the Past. Purification. Be willing to change what needs to be changed. Be coachable. Be forgiving of others and yourself. Don't stay in the same state just because you are afraid to make mistakes. Being idle is the biggest woe. Don't look back, look forward. Use the past errors to have a good kick start. Relaunch your life. Nobody's perfect, make a change.

Ambition is the Fuel to Success. Dream big dreams but make sure you work to put legs on your dreams. Success does not come easy. How much fuel you put into your dreams is what makes a difference. Is it a full tank? Press the accelerator to full speed. Find a good reason to fight for something. What do you want to champion? Who are you fighting for? Who do you want to be?

Surviving Versus Thriving. If you choose to survive you will remain invisible. Being invisible is boring and it hurts. We have a voice. Let us be heard. We are all beautiful creatures of God. Let us be seen. Don't just be a spectator. Dare to be on the stage. You are valuable. You are important. Unleash the power within you. Break through all barriers in life. Find the courage to thrive.

A Life Neutralized by Prayers. Deny arrogance and submit to the higher power that is God. Prayers. Always live a life with utmost prayers. Spirituality is a remarkable gift. Make sure you share that invaluable gift with others. Speak of truth. Speak of life. You will attract the world. You will become an influencer. Do not overlook the Higher Power where you draw your inner strength, for a life neutralized by prayer can move mountains.

Share Your Gifts with Others. A giant tree in an uninhabited jungle, as the saying goes, does not make any noise when it falls. It does not make any noise because, simply, no one hears it fall. A man who lives by and for himself alone would be like a giant tree in the jungle. When he dies, who would miss him? Who would remember him? What would his life be worth? Decide to live for others. Serve others who need help. Give back, for there is joy in giving.

You are the Author of Your Own Life. Take the risks. Don't be afraid to make mistakes. Don't be afraid to face hardships in life. Your experiences will shape you well and prepare you for your journey. Don't be afraid to embrace self-exploration. Travel if you can make it happen. Explore various places. If you are single, stay in a new place every couple of months. Meet new people. Continue to learn. Be hungry for knowledge. Life is short. See the world. See how other people live. Open a new door to the world of possibilities. Don't' set expectations. Take one day at a time. Forge new friendships. Find new mentors. Live life to its fullest, so when it's your time to leave this earth, you have no regrets. Don't be afraid to die. When we are called, we are called. God will welcome us to His Majestic Kingdom. What matters is what mark we left here on earth.

Preparation is essential. It's time to write your own story. It's time to leave a mark on earth. Lock arms with me and together let's inspire this beautiful world we live in. Our stories can make a difference. They change people's lives. I pray and hope that each one of you will carry a huge smile on your face after reading this book. I am smiling at you right now. My heart is filled with bliss! It is purified. I trust yours is too.

You are beautiful inside and out. We all are. We are fearfully and beautifully created by God. Let the fire in your heart burn and let it not die. Let it light up for the rest of your life. Let that light be seen by the world. You, yes you. You are precious. You are valuable. You are dear to me and to God. He is there living in your heart. Listen to your heart. Hush, and listen attentively. Bring out the lion in you. You are ready. You are YOU. There is a LION in everyone's HEART. It is time to transfigure and become a warrior in life. Discover courage and greatness within. **Become a LION AT HEART.**

"Be strong and courageous! Do not be afraid, do not be discouraged, for the Lord your God will be with you wherever you go."

– Joshua 1:9

About the Author

Originally from the Philippines, the youngest of four siblings, Kai Hayes lived an impoverished life. At the age of 25, Kai Hayes became the sole breadwinner for her parents and grandparents. After a short marriage of three years, she became a single mother at the age of 33. With little to no resources, she discovered courage and greatness within.

Her determination to create financial freedom propelled her to overcame numerous barriers in life to become a top corporate executive and established her own telecommunications business in Asia. Recognizing no limits, Kai continued to skyrocket forward and became a successful global entrepreneur in network marketing.

Today, Kai is mother to her only son Nico, two stepchildren Grant and Michelle, and married to the love of her life, Greg. Together, they give back by running the Bridge of Hope Ministry to help orphans and the impoverished children in the Philippines. She is dedicated to helping others achieve health, time, and financial freedom.

Kai Hayes
Kai Hayes Lifestyle YouTube
www.kaihayes.com
Kai Hayes Facebook
Kai Hayes LinkedIn
Kaihayes31@gmail.com

Made in the USA
Middletown, DE
10 April 2023

28437938R00087